EQUALITY VS EQUITY

EQUALITY VS EQUITY

Tackling Issues of Race in the Workplace

BY

JENNY GARRETT OBE
Jenny Garrett Global, UK

emerald PUBLISHING

United Kingdom – North America – Japan – India
Malaysia – China

Emerald Publishing Limited
Howard House, Wagon Lane, Bingley BD16 1WA, UK

First edition 2023

Reprints and permissions service
Contact: permissions@emeraldinsight.com

British Library Cataloguing in Publication Data
A catalogue record for this book is available from the British Library

ISBN: 978-1-80382-676-9 (Print)
ISBN: 978-1-80382-673-8 (Online)
ISBN: 978-1-80382-675-2 (Epub)

Printed and bound by CPI Group (UK) Ltd, Croydon, CR0 4YY

ISOQAR certified
Management System,
awarded to Emerald
for adherence to
Environmental
standard
ISO 14001:2004.

Certificate Number 1985
ISO 14001

INVESTOR IN PEOPLE

PRAISE FOR *EQUALITY VS EQUITY*

'An excellent book for anyone who wants to learn more and truly understand the importance of equity and how to create inclusion through the lens of race. Jenny shares many great examples of her own lived experiences which really help to bring the book to life.'

Asif Sadiq MBE, Chief Diversity, Equity and Inclusion Officer, Warner Bros.

'*Equality vs Equity* is a great work authored through the lived experience lens of specialist coach and trainer in the diversity arena, Jenny Garrett OBE. It is the game changer required to achieve a fresh new approach to challenge a 40-year-old problem. A must have (handbook full) of step-by-step advice for anyone with real commitment and interest in moving the Equality vs Equity Dial forward.'

Dr Yvonne Thompson CBE, DL Chair, Black Cultural Archives

'As usual, I learn from Jenny Garrett OBE every time we interact – this time via her latest fantastic book. Share this hugely practical book with friends, colleagues and others who either want to, or perhaps need to, become more ADEPT at living in a modern world where the global majority deserve far more.'

Dr Suzanne Doyle-Morris, Author of *The Con Job: Getting Ahead for Competence in a World Obsessed with Confidence*

'A book of bountiful evidence and facts on the state of play today in terms of racial equality in UK workplaces. Combining powerful personal experience presented dispassionately with figures and stories from across the recent past, Jenny offers a simple framework to get the reader – who is curious and interested to make a difference – to be part of the solution. A recommended read.'

Sarah Churchman OBE, Chief Inclusion,
Community and Wellbeing Officer, PwC

'If you read one book this year, make it this one! I have worked with Jenny on a number of occasions and always come away having learnt something and with a renewed vigour to make a difference. The fact [that] Jenny has put her unique storytelling abilities, borne of her lived and professional experience, into a book is just a gift to us all. In her introduction, Jenny talks about the African proverb "if you think you are too small to make a difference, you haven't spent the night with a mosquito." I couldn't think of a stronger rally call for everyone to listen, learn and continue making the difference we can [...].'

Gareth Hind, Head of Equality,
Diversity and Inclusion, First Bus

'I never feel that I'm doing enough to understand and tackle racial inequity[.] I don't think it's possible for me or any white person to ever be doing enough in this space. We can all learn more, listen more, hear more and take more action. If, like me, you want to play your part in tackling racial inequity then you really must read this book. It's time to be the Empathetic changemaker the world needs you to be. It's also time we started to accept that those who are Black, Asian, Brown, dual-heritage, indigenous to the global south, and or have been racialised as "ethnic Minorities" are actually, as Jenny explains, the Global Majority. The clock is ticking for those of us white folks, we are the Global Minority, we need to learn fast, and make change happen even faster [...] in the interest of everyone on our little planet.'

Andy Woodfield, PwC Partner,
Global Sector Leader for International Development

'If we're going to tackle racial injustice, then we need to address the fact that there is no such thing as a level playing field, and that the systems in which we live and work are themselves biased and discriminatory. Unless we tackle systemic inequity, there is little chance of achieving racial justice. This book is an important contribution to the field. It helps to increase our understanding and awareness of the systemic injustices at play in our workplaces, organisations and wider systems, and is also a call to all of us to do the work – with guidance on how to become a change-maker, as well as actionable steps we can all take towards greater equity. Most important of all, it stresses the importance of doing our own personal work to enable us to become instruments for change.'

Aboodi Shabi, Lecturer in Coaching and
Behavioural Change, Henley Business School

'I am excited for people to read this book and use it to have moments to have self-reflection, but to also consider the role they play in shifting the dialogue we need to have around race and identity. This is a book for everyone and all. Well done Jenny for continuing this important conversation.'

Geoffrey O. Williams, Global VP of Diversity,
Equity and Inclusion, Burberry

'The combination of Jenny's honest lived experiences, well thought out research and clear explanations of complex topics make this a superbly compelling read. I recommend it for anyone who is afraid to have frank and honest conversations about race and wants to become a better ally.'

Janet Tidmarsh FCIPD

'Jenny Garrett OBE has written a deeply personal, persuasive and highly educational book that will add to the rich, progressive discussion on racial equity and equality in the UK and more widely. This is definitely a must read!'

Peter Alleyne, Associate Director for Diversity,
Equity, Inclusion and Race Equality, Rethink Mental Illness

'This book is an extension of Jenny's passion, honesty and ability to open your thought process and understanding of the world as it equates to racial equity. It's unapologetic, enlightening, yet practical. Jenny is voicing the conversations that your black and brown colleagues are having behind closed doors every day. If you are serious about understanding racial equity and challenging your own assumptions, this book is a "must" read for anyone to actively engage in changing the narrative.'

Devi Virdi, Group Head of Diversity
and Inclusion, Centrica Plc

'Jenny Garrett has written a book that will soon become essential to anyone committed to developing and nurturing equitable workplaces and societies. Jenny draws on her experience in professional and personal spaces to inform how individuals, groups, and societies can become more aware of racial injustices, and she offers practice recommendations that can lead to greater inclusivity. I will be recommending this book to both colleagues and students.'

Professor Carole Elliott, Associate Dean Equality,
Diversity, Inclusion and Development,
Sheffield University Management School

'I met Jenny in the lockdown zone, I mention this because it was a tipping point in the life and history for Black People. Notably we experienced the pandemic, the George Floyd murder, and a global community awakening and awareness. I think this book is timely, it is needed and instructional to make sense of the world we are living in and to help navigate how we move from equality to equity.'

Karl George MBE Partner RSM,
Author of the RACE Equality Code

"Knotty, gordian issues require focused minds and bold actions to unravel them and mobilise change. Jenny Garrett's new book does this honestly, vulnerably and directly to the entrenched issue of racism. With finesse and compelling assuredness, Jenny invites one and all to the table to explore the issue of race justice and to do so from the position of "the solution focused change agent". She compels the reader to state, full throated and unapologetically, that "The Time for change is now. The agent of change is me". Get ready, dear reader, to be equipped, emboldened, and roused to be a powerful catalyst for change.'

Sharon Amesu, Co-Founder, She Leads for Legacy

'This is a much needed book for the current times we are living in. It is extremely well researched with academic references and lived experiences. It is easy to understand and implement as a handbook for every organisation or leader who aspires to be anti-racist. Jenny explains the difference between equality and equity in a way that makes so much sense, while offering practical tips and strategies to achieve true equity in the workplace.'

Wali Rahman, Diversity and Wellbeing Manager, Forestry Commission

'I love Jenny's positive approach. In *Equality vs Equity* Jenny acknowledges that real change is happening and explains why the shift from equality to equity is a vital part of the process if we are to keep up the momentum. I applaud Jenny's positive mindset and progressive nature which make *Equality vs Equity* a must read for anyone who truly wants to understand how to move the dial forward.'

Gamiel Yafai, Founder and CEO, Diversity Marketplace

'I admire and applaud the courage Jenny Garrett demonstrates in raising a variety of issues in this very timely book. Whilst she could have been tempted to quietly enjoy the privileges afforded by her own success, she has chosen the less travelled road of identifying and analysing the very real issues we face, especially in the workplace and related settings. [...] I am certain that those who have values that include ethical and equitable conduct will embrace this book that draws us into deeper reflections about our own practices and conduct and how we can achieve racial equity. I am pleased that Jenny candidly discusses her own journey and the experiences of others as well as what the possibilities for change can be, if we are resilient in our pursuit of racial equity.'

'We can all contribute to the debate – I believe that this book shares a balanced perspective that all of us, from all walks of life and communities, can learn from. I hope that we embrace the many lessons and take time to reflect on our own values, beliefs and practices as we read this book with the view to as Jenny says, "seeing differently, thinking differently and doing things differently". [...] Together we can create a truly better tomorrow for us all.'

Dr Irene Brew-Riverson, Senior Lecturer,
University of Westminster

'An engaging and relatable read that had me gripped from the beginning, *Equality vs Equity* helps readers grasp the concept of racial equity in its true essence through practical and action-oriented strategies — a must-read for those serious about understanding and implementing racial equity at work.'

Hira Ali, Founder of Advancing Your Potential
and Author *of Her Way To The Top: A Guide to
Smashing the Glass Ceiling* and *Her Allies: A Practical
Toolkit to Help Men Lead Through Advocacy*

'The conversation on racial inequality in the UK has progressed over the last few years but there is still much to do, learn and be implemented in order to make real progress on this agenda. *Equality vs Equity: Tackling Issues of Race in the Workplace* is the tool we've been waiting for that provides really helpful guidance and practical solutions [for] an ongoing issue and for organisations willing to make the change. I really do recommend reading this!'

Sharniya Ferdinand, Diversity, Equity and Inclusion Consultant

'Jenny has achieved through this book a brilliant work of authentically narrating her lived experiences, intricately woven persuasive arguments about the urgency of amplifying equity and providing actionable strategies for anyone. Each chapter is steeped in history, research, anecdotes, and practical tools to kindle one's desire for action. This is a must read for anyone interested in contributing to creating an equitable future in business and society at large.'

Dr Jummy Okoya, Senior Lecturer and Chair,
Women's Network, University of East London

'Jenny has been challenging and shaping equality in the workplace for many years and as a result is a leader in this space. I have witnessed leaders change their internal processes as a result of her delivery and heard employees reflect on the impact they can have following her sessions. I know that this book will have a huge impact on every reader and will continue to shape ED&I globally.'

Sonia Meggie, Diversity and Inclusion Consultant

'The narrative around racial equity has always been uncomfortable in the workplace; made even more difficult when you include the many layers of intersectionality. [...] After nearly two decades of [...] debate, this book will offer a fresh insight into racial bias and discrimination, and how leaders can become more comfortable and, more importantly, diligent change makers rather than [...] complacent managers sitting on the side-lines expecting change.'

Sonia Brown MBE, Founder and Director,
National Black Women's Network (NBWN) and SistaTalk

'In this book Jenny has provided an easy, informative, and engaging resource that bridges the gap between awareness for race equality, and the practical steps we must all take to ensure race equity. This is not just another book about race, this is a playbook that will shift gears for race equity, from conversation to action to long term impact!'

Pauline Miller, Chief Equity Officer EMEA,
Dentsu International

To my wonderful caring and patient family and friends, in particular my husband, mum, daughter, and goddaughter who came on the writing journey with me and inspire me daily. A special thanks to those busy people who made time to be interviewed for this book, I appreciate you.

CONTENTS

INTRODUCTION

I write this book from a place of hope, optimism, and progress. Although the pace of change is not fast enough, and some may doubt the sustainability or true commitment of organisations to diversity, equity, and inclusion. Real change has happened over the last two years. In every sphere, the topic of racial equality is being discussed from the media to politics, in living rooms around the country, the classroom, and in your organisation. The challenge is to sustain the momentum and build on it with irreversible action. I truly believe that this can be achieved when we join together. As the African proverb goes 'If you think you are too small to make a difference, you haven't spent the night with a mosquito'. If each one of us chooses to unite in positive action what may seem hopeless and insurmountable can be overcome.

To achieve racial equity in the workplace, we need to become ADEPT by:

expanding our **A**wareness of the context,
Deepening our knowledge of lived experience,
being an **E**mpathetic changemaker,
defining our **P**athways to action,
and practicing **T**houghtful introspection.

This book will help you unpack the concept of racial equity and understand its importance in moving the dial on inclusion, providing language, and practical tips for you to take action. It is essential reading for HR professionals, leaders, and those who want to educate themselves and influence others to do the crucial complex work of achieving racial equity in the workplace.

I want to start by answering the question that you may have which is 'Why a book on racial equity when there are so many issues to focus on including sexism, ableism, homophobia, and classism to name a few?' The truth is that there is no single-issue challenge, all are important and intersect with each other, and are worth focussing on individually and together.

Conversations around diversity and inclusion have tripled in the last year and Diversity and Inclusion roles are growing 1.65 times faster than HR roles in Europe, the Middle East, and Africa according to LinkedIn, the world's largest professional network on the internet. Yet, in the UK, we seem to find the subject of race and racial justice hardest to talk about, according to findings from the Business in the Community report 2021, 59% of employees are still uncomfortable talking about race in UK workplaces. You may have been trying to educate yourself in the equality, diversity, and inclusion space, and felt overwhelmed by initiatives, and time pressured in your day job, this book is *an accessible resource to guide you through that journey.*

It's likely that you will have a woman in your family, know someone who identifies as having a visible or invisible disability, have a friend who is from the lesbian, gay, bisexual, transgender, intersex, queer/questioning, asexual + community but you may not be close to someone who has a different ethnicity to you, and as a result you may not have considered that their lived experience may be very different to your own or had conversations that discuss race and ethnicity.

The strategies within this book can be used beyond racial equity to create wider fairness and inclusion for all in your organisation and beyond.

My desire is for us not to compete in the oppression Olympics and argue about which groups are more ill-treated, instead my goal is for all of us to understand that solutions and a fairer society are what we all seek. In fact, what if we could hold the view that for everyone to win, no one had to lose? It might radically change things.

Within these pages, I use the term 'people of the **global majority**'[1] to describe the myriad of people from Black, Asian, and ethnic
minority backgrounds in the UK. You may be familiar with other
terms, including BAME, those from underrepresented communities, those who are a visible minority, people of colour, African dias-
pora, and those who are from ethnically diverse backgrounds. This
is a diverse group of people who really can't be grouped together,
and so the limitations of language do not do them justice, but this
is what I have settled on for now. The global majority refers to
people who are Black, Asian, Brown, dual heritage, indigenous to
the global south, and/or have been racialised as 'ethnic minorities'.
Globally, these groups currently represent approximately 80% of
the world's population making them the global majority now, and
with current growth rates, notwithstanding COVID-19 and its
emerging variants, the global majority is set to remain so for the
foreseeable future. The language is evolving and may have evolved
by the time you are reading this book, if so, I ask you to forgive me
and see beyond it and look for the learning.

MY LIVED EXPERIENCE

I want to start by acknowledging that I am my ancestors' wildest
dreams. I am one of the only 500 people each year who has received
the Queen's honour of Officer of the Most Excellent Order of the
British Empire (OBE). I have my own home, am university educated, and have a successful business. I am filled with gratitude for
these things, while also understanding that they do not make me
immune to experiencing racial bias and experiencing obstacles in
my journey that others may not.

I am alive to the challenges of achieving racial equity in the
workplace, through my lived experience as a Black British woman
and through my leadership development work with organisations
over almost two decades I have personally listened to the struggles
of hundreds of executives from the global majority who are trying
to navigate and realise their potential in the world of work in the
UK. I have also run focus groups and team coaching sessions for
white leaders, who in the UK are usually, but not always white men,

who have shared their fears of saying or doing the wrong thing, and how that keeps them paralysed from taking action. I have also seen organisations clumsily set targets and make public statements that could be deemed *performative*, they look like they are doing the right thing, when they haven't done the work to truly commit to doing what they think is right or know what that is for them. There is a huge amount of work to be done. However, I am pleased to say some companies are doing the work, attempting to make change, and taking brave steps, we'll talk more about that in Chapter Four.

As a Black woman born and growing up in the UK with Caribbean heritage, I found myself in majority white spaces a lot, from the Girl Guides to the Catholic school I attended, I was one of less than a handful of Black people present.

Because of my complexion, medium brown skin, and green eyes, I wasn't necessarily called names about being Black. I most likely benefitted from **colourism**. Colourism has been around for centuries and is 'thought to be a lasting relic of slavery; white masters showed preferential treatment to light-skinned or mixed-race slaves' says Sociologist Meeta Jha. She adds that 'physical attractiveness, whiteness, and youthfulness have accrued capital, just as darker skin colour, hair texture, disability and ageing have devalued feminine currency'. So, the term that was banded at me was 'half-caste', an incorrect racial slur, but slur nonetheless, I recall being called this up until my twenties. At the time, it was the term often used to describe those of mixed heritage, I thought that it meant to have one parent who was white and one parent who was from the global majority. However, the root of 'half-caste' is the Latin word 'castus', meaning pure, and its Spanish and Portuguese derivatives 'casta', meaning race. So 'half-caste' means impure, it means white is pure and anything else just muddies the blood. So, it was even more offensive than I realised at the time.

I found myself feeling different in lots of ways, my build and physique seemed much bigger than the other girls at school, although when I tell people this now, they seem shocked because, I am average height at 5ft 4 and a half, with a small build. Maybe I grew quickly, and others caught up. My hair was also a source of difference, afro hair styles are steeped in tradition, styles would be used to express our status, whether or not we were married and if we had been through puberty and should be a source of pride, but instead my kinky coily afro hair, was a source of curiosity, from the cornrows to the braids and then the chemical straightening, my hair was different. It was only in 2019 that The CROWN Act[2] was created to ensure protection against discrimination based on race-based hairstyles in the USA. There is no similar law in the UK specifically banning hairstyle discrimination. But this does not mean that there is no issue with this in the UK. There have been a small number of UK cases alleging hairstyle discrimination, including where an employee was told her natural hairstyle was inherently 'untidy' and unprofessional, and a High Court case in 2011, where a child was excluded from school for having cornrows.[3] However, in October 2022, the Equality and Human Rights Commission (EHRC) shared new guidance that pupils should not be stopped from wearing their hair in natural Afro styles at school. Speak to anyone with afro hair working in the UK and they will have a story to tell. Whether it's comments on looking unprofessional, being asked if their hair can be touched, or if their hair belongs to them, they are made to feel like a curiosity at best and at worst as an excuse to be dehumanised. As Emma Dabiri[4] shares the texture of black hair was used as a 'justification' for the enslavement of Africans between the sixteenth and the nineteenth centuries. Emma's research found: 'One of the examples of this [justification] was "look they don't even have hair" – European people have hair. They have wool. Animals have wool. They're more like livestock'.

One incident that sticks with me, aged 12, is sitting at the bus stop to go to school and a white man, probably in his 50's, who appeared to have a blue-collar role, such as builder or plumber, driving a nondescript white van stopping to shout 'Black bitch' at me before continuing with his day, while of course totally ruining mine.

My Mum (who became a schoolteacher while I was in my teens) brought me up to speak 'properly', no slang, no dropping my 'h's' and this helped, it helped me to be accepted and assimilate to a degree. I would get comments from people who would meet me the first time after speaking to me on the phone and be shocked that I wasn't how they had visualised me, telling me 'How surprisingly articulate I was', I now recognise this as a **microaggression,** but I didn't at the time. We'll talk more about microaggressions in Chapter Two.

In the world of work, I did OK. I carried on oblivious to a lot of bias and discrimination. I was sometimes told by white colleagues, you should have got that opportunity but they're racist, but I didn't let it bother me. Sometimes, I found that someone just really didn't like me, when I couldn't ascertain why, I absorbed it and accepted injustice as just the way things were.

I am Black, I am a woman, and I had a working class start. The intersection of these identities really created a feeling of *otherness* for me, particularly in one place I worked which was mostly public school educated white colleagues. I often had no idea what my colleagues were talking about, their lives and upbringing were so different to mine, and I often felt excluded inadvertently and sometimes very directly. I have one memory of working in a small team where there was a high-profile sought-after event that my line manager had one ticket for someone to attend, in turn she asked everyone but me, it stung to be excluded and ignored in this way. Looking back, I should have asked why, I think that I would now, but at the time, it was like school, everyone wants a ticket to that party, and you are waiting to be invited. It's like that a lot when you are "the only" one.

I have heard the saying 'Diversity is being invited to the party and inclusion is being asked to dance' but some of us aren't even invited! Imagine how I felt when one of my colleagues brought up my exclusion to me (as if I hadn't noticed). I just sucked it up and carried on working there. So if I had become angry and unmotivated you could not blame me, could you?

One of the worst experiences I had was speaking at a conference and then attending the evening gala dinner. I was sat opposite an older white gentleman who first asked me if I was catering staff, even though I was sitting opposite him and dressed in an evening gown. He then proceeded to ask me where I went on holiday, when I answered that I like to see the world and don't have a particular place that I go back to, I was then asked whether 'I go back to my own country regularly', followed by a string of comments about going back and staying there. Others around us squirmed in their seats and tried to veer him off his mission to make me feel like I didn't belong, yet no one acted as **ally** and intervened, stood up for me, or called him out. Typical **passive bystander** behaviour took place, and it was a painful experience, in a work environment. The interesting thing was that the following year I spoke at the same event and saw the same person, he didn't recall how rude and offensive he'd been to me, but the memory stays with me.

Three chapters into writing this book, I attended a networking event at a prestigious City of London venue. I was talking to a connection of mine, a tall white man who is inclusive and open, we were in mid conversation and a white woman who looked like she was in her early 60's interrupted and introduced herself to him. She evidently had no intention of introducing herself to me, so I assertively held out a hand and introduced myself, forcing her to acknowledge me. She shook my hand and told me I was beautiful and got back to her talk with my connection. This sounds like a compliment, but it wasn't, it was 'if I give you a compliment, I can get back to talking important stuff with the important person next to you'. As I watched her network throughout the evening, she was talking to everyone she decided looked like they were powerful and influential and ignoring everyone else. If I was a less confident, resilient person, I could have taken her behaviour quite badly, maybe felt like I didn't belong, didn't have much worth, and gone home early. Instead, I shrugged it off, but I am clear that a **microaggression**, can look like a compliment, 'You are articulate, you are beautiful, you are intelligent, that should placate you while I speak to the people that really matter' the equivalent of 'You're pretty for a Black girl'. My connection was gracious and knew that her behaviour was at the very least rude, he made a passing comment about it, and we moved on. It was subtle enough not to challenge directly, but not subtle enough not to leave a bad feeling.

The struggle is real, the struggle is ongoing, and the struggle is rarely visible. No one should suck it up, no one should be made to feel inferior, and people should be able to realise their potential. It's time for change and YOU can make it happen.

How often do you watch the news and say, 'oh that's sad, but what can I do about it' or 'that's depressing I think I'll stop watching because it's bringing me down'? This is your chance to make a difference in a practical way, take the blinkers off, stop numbing yourself to the situation, and be the change! I believe in the goodness of people and that you personally and intentionally can change things and this book will help you work out how.

HOW TO READ THIS BOOK

We are all at different points of our journey and I wrote this book with the intention for you to read it cover to cover; however, you may want to dive in at a particular chapter, which will work well too. Underpinning all I do is the foundation of being a coach, so please note my calls to action and reflection, you may want to read the book as a team, or with your peers and discuss it together, this will help you develop your thinking and your ability to speak about these topics. Reading books is great, taking action makes it meaningful.

In Chapter One, 'Awareness of Context', you will learn about the evolution of equality and the growing importance of equity. This chapter explores the current state of the UK workplace in terms of equality and equity and how we got here, and how far we still must go.

In Chapter Two, 'Deepening Our Knowledge of Lived Experience', you will gain insight into the racially inequitable workplace. Through stories, you will then be given an insight into the lived workplace experience of those from the global majority and their experience of inequity.

In Chapter Three, 'Being an Empathetic Changemaker', you will gain understanding on how to be a changemaker. This chapter identifies what stops individuals (often white leaders) from tackling racial inequity, pitfalls that they can experience when they try, and strategies to move forward.

In Chapter Four, 'Defining Our Pathways to Action', you will consider actionable steps to disrupting the workplace system. This chapter will provide you with practical actions that can be taken organisationally to advance equity in the workplace which include: ascertaining collective knowledge, bringing to light your blind spots, learning from your colleagues, and experimenting to find out what works for you and your organisation.

In Chapter Five, 'Practising Thoughtful Introspection', you will focus on doing the personal work necessary to advance equity in your professional life. This chapter is for those wish to do some soul searching and deeper work to uncover their motivations, fears, and goals around racial equity. You will gain personal strategies to develop the ability to champion equity in the workplace.

Lastly, we have a glossary of terms for your reference. You will find all of the words emboldened in the text defined within the glossary.

Notes

1. Global Majority coined by Rosemary Campbell-Stephens MBE.

2. CROWN Act by Dove and the CROWN Coalition, in partnership with then State Senator Holly J. Mitchell of California.

3. *G v Head Teacher and Governors of St Gregory's Catholic Science College.*

4. Dabiri, E. (2020, 5 March). *Don't touch my hair.* Penguin.

Chapter One

AWARENESS OF CONTEXT

EQUALITY VS EQUITY

'When it comes to racial equality at work, it is important that businesses know the difference between equality and equity' said Labour MP David Lammy.[1]

David Lammy acknowledged that 'In a post-George-Floyd/ Black Lives Matter [society], there is more acceleration on the issue of racial injustice' but highlighted that the 'business of equity' is crucial in understanding 'where people are starting from' when it comes to diversity in the workplace.

Whatever your political leanings, it's good news that prominent figures in UK society are talking about equity rather than equality. Striving for equality can provide the illusion that the work of equality can be done through implementing a policy or running an initiative and then going back to the way you always did things. This work is not 'one and done' it needs to be embedded and ongoing.

After all, over the last 800 years there have been national and international milestones that have shaped the concept of human rights in Britain none of which have eliminated racism. From the Magna Carta in 1215 which acknowledged for the first time that subjects of the Crown had legal rights and that laws could apply to kings and queens too, to the Race Relations Act of 1965. This was the first legislation in the UK to address racial discrimination. Although it was criticised because it only covered discrimination in specified public places, the act laid the foundations for more effective legislation. It also set up the Race Relations Board to consider complaints brought under the act. The most recent milestone is the Equality Act 2010 which brought together more than 116 separate pieces of legislation into one single act – a new, streamlined legal framework to protect the rights of individuals and advance equality of opportunity for all. Yet, still equity has not been achieved. Racism, harassment, and victimisation have not been eradicated, even if many have congratulated themselves on the various pieces of legislation that have been created. In fact, it can be argued, that this legislation best serves white colleagues as it protects everyone from discrimination, harassment, and victimisation and those with more power and racial privilege are more likely to be successful in their appeals or cases.

The issue is that racism is ever-present, shape-shifting, and constant and therefore it takes vigilance and **interest convergence** for change to take place. In the workplace, it might look like being told by senior managers that one of your key performance indicators is focussed on the retention and acceleration of team members from the global majority, or it might be that you view yourself as a good person and so you want to support your colleagues from the global majority because that aligns with who you are, or that you've read the research on how creativity and the ability to be competitive increase when you have a more diverse team and want to benefit from that. In these situations, both the white colleagues and those from the global majority are winners.

Instead of striving for racial equality, we should strive for equity, which is:

> A *mindset and method for solving problems that have endured for generations, seem intractable, harm people and communities of colour most acutely, and ultimately affect people of all races. [It] requires seeing differently, thinking differently, and doing the work differently. Racial equity is about results that make a difference and last.*[2]

Through racial equity, the needs of each community, group, or individual are met and everyone benefits from a more just, equitable system.

Racial equity is a step towards **racial justice,** a vision and transformation of society to eliminate racial hierarchies and advance collective freedom where those from the global majority, in particular, but not only, have the dignity, resources, power, and self-determination to fully thrive.

HOW EQUALITY AND EQUITY DIFFER

Equality	Equity
Treat everyone the same	Consider systems that disadvantage and seek to overcome them
Collective approach	Individual approach
Needs management	Needs leadership
Hold power	Share power
Input driven	Outcomes driven

As Lammy points out, equity isn't synonymous with equality. In my experience companies are striving for workplace equality, the idea of treating everyone the same, without discrimination and have not factored in the need for equity. Their aim is for the entire workforce to come under the same blanket of rules, privileges, and employee experience design, without an eye on unique, demographic-related needs. Perversely this may lead to the opposite outcome and actually create an unfair work environment.

Organisations that I spoke to were reticent to just focus on racial equity as they saw it as part of a broader inclusion agenda. They felt that there would be a backlash to focussing just on race and ethnicity as it doesn't impact everyone and may alienate some groups. They were clear that everyone should be committed to racial equity alongside all other types of equity and that the work should transcend an individual or team but be part of the organisation's DNA and truly embedded in all they do. 'Equity can be confronting' said one senior leader, and that it challenged the idea of **meritocracy;** the idea that we all succeed and fail on our own merit, that hard work alone will help us prevail. I believe that this argument is holding back progress, ask yourself why you can discuss gender, disability, and the rights of the LGBTQ+ community without experiencing the same push back.

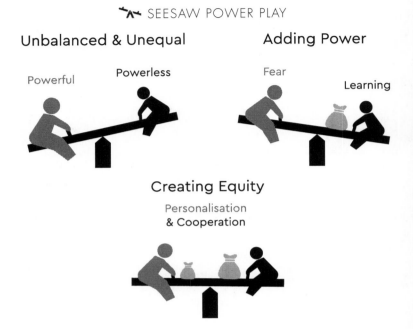

⋏ SEESAW POWER PLAY

Unbalanced & Unequal   Adding Power

Powerful   Powerless   Fear
                                        Learning

Creating Equity

Personalisation
& Cooperation

Let's explore this some more. I think of racial equity in terms of a seesaw, you'll recall a seesaw has a long, narrow board which is fixed in the middle a little way above the ground.

Children often like to play on seesaws. Two children sit on the seesaw, one at each end. The child who is down pushes the ground with their feet so that they go up and their friend goes down. Then the friend pushes up, so the first child goes down. They continue to go back and forth until they are ready to stop playing on the seesaw.

It's most fun with two children who are about the same height and have similar weights. If one child weighs more, then they have the power, they can sit tight and the child at the other end is left high and dry, if they jump off the seesaw suddenly the child goes down with a bump and can hurt themselves. The child who weighs less is at their mercy. The one with weight and power can choose to be kind and gentle or rough, even if they start off gently, they could forget the power that their weight gives. To create equity, we need to even them up, the child who weighs more could dispose of some of their weight, if that were healthy and possible, or we could add some weight on the other child's side, to even things up, which is most practical.

If we decide to even things up with a few sandbags, the child who had all of the power because they weighed more may fear losing the power that they enjoyed or worse still that the other child may now have the advantage, which could leave them feeling vulnerable, or like they might be repaid for times they weren't a considerate playmate.

Once they both have equal weight, they can now work together to decide how they distribute it, to do this they must appreciate what each other brings even if it's different, and that could include different ways of thinking, as well as being and doing. At this point, they must decide on the push and pull needed to achieve the outcomes that they both want.

There is more to this picture though, both of the children have to have access and entry to the play park in the first place, the sandbags have to be available, the child shouldn't be labelled a troublemaker as soon as they walk in, and they should be afforded the same compassion as the others playing if they fall and hurt themselves. The idea of equity is that we can even things up so that they can both enjoy the seesaw and share the power.

It's important to acknowledge that the child with the weight and power advantage did not choose to have it and of course in some situations their partner on the seesaw might be heavier than them, but it's also about recognising when you are the heaviest and increasing your awareness about what you need to do to even things up and use your advantage positively.

What typically happens in the workplace is that the well-meaning manager gives both colleagues equal sandbags, and just perpetuates the imbalance that exists. Looking through an equity lens changes things.

Racial equity is not just about us having equity of opportunity but equity of outcomes too, irrespective of whether you have the weight advantage on the seesaw, we should both be able to have fun on it. What happens in the workplace is that those from the global majority are given support to think their way to equal power, while the person guarding the sandbags (which in the workplace equate to stretch opportunities, invitations to network, sponsorship, exposure to senior people and different parts of the business, opportunities to shadow and deputise, being heard, being acknowledged, and appreciated for who you are) stands watching and not distributing. Even when the sandbags are distributed to create equity, there is a mindset shift needed in both parties' learning, how to use that weight when that they haven't had it before, and how to let go of having all of the advantage without resentment by the other party.

Forward thinking diversity, equity, and inclusion professionals are doing this work.

I'm doing the work to make sure that I am creating the same outcomes for everyone in our organisation, regardless of their starting point. It's where we're removing the barriers that create things that restrict us from being equal and equitable across our business. (Geoffrey Williams, Vice President/Global Head Diversity & Inclusion, Burberry)

You should be able to reach your potential no matter your background. Equity leads to Inclusion, it's a bridge to unlocking talent and therefore increasing retention, innovation, and creativity. (Janet Tidmarsh, FCIPD)

Equity in Action

Let's take an example. You as a leader have a conference in another country that you can choose two colleagues to attend. You choose one colleague from the global majority and one white colleague to attend, you see them both as high-performing, this is equality.

However, if we are using the equity lens, you might have a conversation with each of them to understand what might get in the way of a successful trip and out of that conversation could come responses such as:

- I always get searched at the airport; I may need longer to through than my colleague does, can we adjust the itinera.

- I will need time to research to make sure that there aren't areas that are dangerous for people like me.

- Can I still adhere to my religious beliefs and rituals while taking the trip?

- Can we ensure people know what I look like before I get there, so I don't have to deal with surprised facial expressions or being mistaken for someone less senior?

Following the conversation, you could work together to put in place what is necessary to even the seesaw as much as possible, or the colleague may make a choice not to attend the conference and not be penalised for it because you understand the reasons why.

THE MYTH OF MERITOCRACY

Some will question, why do they deserve the sandbags, I got my weight/power on merit. I ate well and grew strong and tall, it's not my fault that genetically you are lighter and smaller. This is an important argument. How do we define merit, if they are genetically predisposed to being taller and heavier or have more opportunities to be in the fresh air and eat good food? Is this real merit or luck, due to the life that they have been born into?

This may go against all you believe, especially if your mantra is 'if you work hard enough, you will succeed'. But **meritocracy** is a myth, the idea that through determination and hard work, alone, we can pull ourselves up by our bootstraps is frankly not true, none of us are self-made, we all stand on the shoulders of giants. Maybe there are times in your workplace where an unlikely candidate secured a role, or a role was created for someone, or you've seen blatant nepotism, all indications that we are not a meritocracy. There are the examples of those from the global majority who succeed beyond the odds, even when they do their position can remain tenuous without the safety net that others may have.

As a result of this meritocracy myth, those from the global majority may believe that if they are not successful then they must be lazy, stupid, or incompetent and deserve what they have or don't have. But the experience for many, though not all people from the global majority, is more complicated. Factors such as **institutional racism**, education level of family members, and access to fewer resources that help them succeed means that many of their paths to personal success are challenging in more ways than their white counterparts.

I see the picture time and time again, that bright new starters join an organisation sometimes 50% of a new intake or higher from the global majority and they meet a broken rung on the career ladder or hit a concrete ceiling rather than a glass ceiling that stops them moving further at the same rate as their white counterparts. Take a look at your organisation, the following image represents a pattern that I have seen with few exceptions in the UK and beyond. Good representation at junior levels and representation of those from the global majority rapidly declining as we go up the ranks, in reality the picture is often starker than this, with less than 5% of the senior leaders from the global majority overall in the UK. Ask for the picture in your organisation and compare.

How Global Majority Representation Typically Declines at Senior Levels

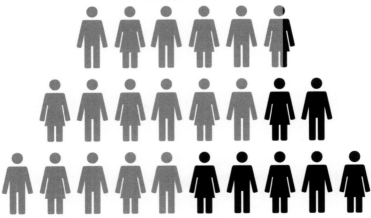

The truth is that **racial privilege** *or advantage* due to race *is* what helps you succeed in an unjust society. Note that those from the global majority can have privilege too, it just won't be racial privilege in the UK.

The wonderful news is that if you discover that you have racial privilege you can use it for good, don't feel shame, guilt, or a casualty of your circumstance which is disabling, but instead think of how you'll use your power positively, to amplify others, to challenge the system, to bridge the gaps, to bring those outside in, to balance the seesaw, to negotiate the push and pull, and to remove the park gates to make the seesaw accessible to all.

A senior diversity, equity, and inclusion expert sums up equity beautifully:

'*We must remove each and every condition that leads to unequal outcomes*'.

Tips to Advance Racial Equity

- Take an individual approach to lead your colleagues and understand their needs.

- Start to share your power, a first step could be rotating the chairing of a meeting or asking for others' opinions.

- Become curious about what is getting in the way of your colleague's success.

RACE IN RECENT TIMES IN THE UK

Postmodern Racism intersects with many other aspects of discrimination and power imbalances. (Senior DEI Leader)

You may have noticed a shift in your colleagues from the global majority over the last two years. An increase in uncomfortable conversations around race, ethnicity, and racism. I visited a school recently to deliver a talk in their assembly for International Women's Day, which was one of the highlights of my year, and the deputy head who was a white middle-aged, middle-class man chatted with me. We happened on the topic of diversity, equity, and inclusion, and he told me about the journey he had been and was still on to educate himself and become more aware of his biases and racial privilege. He said that a year ago he would have found the conversation deeply uncomfortable, now it was just mildly uncomfortable and that he wanted friends to be patient with him as he was learning and growing as fast as he could. I really appreciated his perspective on patience, combined with my impatience for change. It's important when you are already far along in this journey that you are patient with those catching up, your irritation with them can slow their journey. A bit like when you weren't grasping a topic quickly enough in school and the schoolteacher showed their impatience and as a result you just closed down. That doesn't mean that I think that change should slow down, just that we must meet people where they are in their journey.

I find that people immediately think I am talking about racism when I mention race and I think that race and ethnicity are often confused. To feel confident in these conversations about race, ethnicity, and racism, we at the very least should have an understanding of these terms. So, I share definitions here to help you feel confident in the conversations that I know you will be having.

Race is a social construct, a grouping system created by humans. Race was invented as a means of outlining physical differences between people, with one group classified as superior to another. Race forms the basis of white being superior to the global majority and there is no biological or psychological evidence to support this. The concept of race has been used to oppress and justify differential treatment. In fact, some groups, such as Italians that are considered 'white' in the USA today were considered 'non-white' in previous eras.

Ethnicity refers to large groups of people classed according to common racial, national, tribal, religious, linguistic, or cultural origin or background, a social construct used to categorise and characterise seemingly distinct populations. Everyone has an ethnicity, and 'white British' is an ethnic group.[3] Bhavnani et al. (2005, p. 213) point out that it is common in British culture for 'ethnic' to be wrongly used as synonymous with non-white or not western, for example, with 'ethnic clothes' or 'ethnic restaurants'.

Racism, the 'R' word that no one wants to be accused of, again involves one group having the power to carry out systematic discrimination through the institutional policies and practices of the society and by shaping the cultural beliefs and values that support those racist policies and practices. Think of the seesaw and who holds the weight. Racism does not have to be deliberate. **Critical Race Theory (CRT)** thinking is that racism is so commonplace that we don't see it, just like the air around us, and this leads to **colourblindness** and the belief that we are a **meritocracy**.

These conversations that you may have had at work regarding, race, ethnicity, and racism may have unlocked a door to your colleagues from the global majority's stories, personal experiences with race and racism, including **intergenerational pain** and trauma, many they may not have had the safe space and courage to reveal before, and a realisation of the inequity in UK society.

According to government statistics, the experience of those from the global majority in the UK[4] is listed as follows:

- People from the global majority make up 14.4% of the UK (16.1% for England, 5.9% for Wales, 5.4% for Scotland, and 2.2% for Northern Ireland).

- The unemployment rate for Black people was 13.8% compared to 4.5% for white people from October to December 2020, up from 8.7% and 3.4% for the same period in 2019.

- Overall, 28% of people in Black households are on a persistent low income compared to 12% in white households.

- Nearly 27% of Black people live in overcrowded accommodation compared to 8.3% of white people.

- Only 20% of Black African and 40% of Black Caribbean households own their own homes compared to 68% of white British.

- Black graduates earn about 23% less on average than white graduates and are almost twice as likely to be unemployed as their white peers a year after leaving college.

- Black people are underrepresented in senior positions. There are no Black executives in any of the top three roles in FTSE 100 companies.

Of course, Black people are just one ethnicity within those from the global majority, but these stats paint a picture of the seesaw not being tipped in their favour.

Let's explore some examples of what inequity looks like from recent times. The *Windrush Lessons Learned Review*[5] was updated in 2022 nearly two years since the scandal hit the headlines.

The review makes absolutely clear that the Windrush scandal was not an accident, but the inevitable result of policies designed to make life impossible for those without the right papers. Black people who had been invited to come to the UK, who worked and lived in the UK and called it home were being sent back to the Caribbean, my own mother, a retired school teacher who has lived in the UK since she was 13 years old, searched for her papers to ensure that she was a UK citizen and couldn't be sent back to a place that hasn't been home for over half a century. The fear of being taken from her family, home, friends at the whim of the UK government was heart wrenching.

This, coupled with decades of immigration legislation explicitly aimed at reducing non-white immigration from the Commonwealth, destroyed the lives of many people from the global majority.

There was widespread shock and outrage at the fact that so many Black Britons had had their lives devastated by Britain's deeply flawed and discriminatory immigration system.

The government acknowledged its failings, far too late for many, and The Windrush Compensation Scheme was designed to right the wrongs of the Windrush scandal although delays and difficulties in applying for the Scheme have compounded those injustices.

The killing of George Floyd an African American man at the hands of a police officer in Minneapolis caused global uproar in 2020. Maybe it resonated because we were all at home due to the COVID-19 global pandemic, or the fact that it was on video meant that could see for ourselves and the behaviour couldn't be explained away as it might have been otherwise, combined with the rise of social media's heightened feeling around how appalling it was. I say this because sadly George Floyd is not the first case of this kind, and although many UK residents believe that this doesn't happen at home, I can name just a few, for example, Cynthia Jarrett in 1985, Cherry Groce in 1985, Joy Gardner in 1993, and Stephen Lawrence a Black British teenager from Plumstead, southeast London, who was murdered in a racially motivated attack while waiting for a bus in 1993, when he was 18 years old. His death was not at the hands of the police, but it did take two police investigations and a public inquiry to gain convictions. Then we lost Roger Sylvester in 1999, Jimmy Mubenga in 2010, Smiley Culture in 2011, Mark Duggan in 2011, Julian Cole in 2013, Mzee Mohammed-Daley in 2016, Sarah Reed in 2016, and Trevor Smith in 2019 who died in police custody, or at the hands of those who were supposed to protect and serve them in the UK.

During the first wave of the COVID-19 global pandemic (24 January 2020 to 11 September 2020), people from the global majority (except for women in the Chinese or 'white Other' ethnic groups) had higher rates of death involving the coronavirus compared with the White British population.

The rate of death involving COVID-19 was highest for the Black African group (3.7 times greater than for the white British group for males and 2.6 greater for females), followed by the Bangladeshi (3.0 for males and 1.9 for females), Black Caribbean (2.7 for males and 1.8 for females), and Pakistani (2.2 for males and 2.0 for females) ethnic groups.[6]

Some of the reasons for this were found to be that many people from these communities often had roles as frontline workers, in fact, just over a quarter of dental practitioners, medical practitioners, and opticians are from the global majority. They were also more likely to be nurses, medical radiographers, nursing auxiliaries and assistants, and technicians. So they had more exposure to COVID-19. The Office for National Statistics (ONS) also found from deaths data that, of working men, Black and Asian men were more likely to work in occupations that have had a higher risk of death involving COVID-19. Bangladeshi and Pakistani men make up around a third of taxi drivers and chauffeurs in the UK, and there are other services where the global majority have a relatively high proportion of jobs, such as security and cleaning. Lastly many people from the global majority lived in built-up areas, at the time of the last census. Where rural areas were comprised of 97.5% white and 2.5% the global majority (excluding white minorities), urban areas were comprised of 83.3% white and 16.7% the global majority (excluding white minorities). Thinking about the seesaw, we can visualise why in this situation the distribution of weight was crucial, allowing those not at risk to distribute their power to those who were. Although this didn't necessarily take place.

Farcically, in the midst of this the UK Prime Minister's office much-delayed report by its Commission on Race and Ethnic Disparities in March 2022 suggested that the UK should be seen as model of racial equality. This report provoked a disappointed and angry response from race equality experts describing it as 'extremely disturbing' and offensive to frontline workers from the global majority who had died in disproportionate numbers during the global pandemic in the UK. In many ways, this sums up the UK attitude, which is that racism happens elsewhere, but not in the UK. The UK no longer has signs like 'no Irish, no Blacks, no dogs' on Bed & Breakfast windows as it did in the 1960s but that does not make those from the global majority free from systemic and covert racial inequity.

In March 2022, news broke of Child Q, as the girl is known, a 15-year Black London schoolgirl who was removed from an exam and made to take off her clothes while she was on her period with no adult teacher present. The incident took place in December 2020 after a teacher wrongly accused the girl of possessing cannabis. The girl naturally experienced trauma from the event and is said to be having counselling. Sadly, this was not a one-off incident, it has emerged that 25 intimate searches were carried out on children in one year in the borough of Hackney, sparking fears that this is becoming a widespread practice in diverse and multicultural schools across Britain. Of those 25 strip-searches, 23 were Black, and in almost all cases nothing incriminating was found. An official investigation into the Child Q case found that racism and **adultification,** where adults perceive Black children as being older than they are, were contributing factors.

The Local Child Safeguarding Practice Review in March 2022 found:

> *Having considered the context of the incident, the views of those engaged in the review and the impact felt by Child Q and her family, racism (whether deliberate or not) was likely to have been an influencing factor in the decision to undertake a strip search.*

What if that had been your daughter, niece, sister, friends' child? If we have bias in our schools, we have bias in society and if we have bias in society, we most definitely have bias in your place of work.

Most recently, we have heard reports of the inhuman way that Black people fleeing war in Ukraine have faced racism. For African students lured to Ukraine by the prospect of jobs and university degrees, being treated like economic migrants, rather than refugees displaced by war, was a devastating blow.

In July 2020, the Black Equity Organisation[7] was founded, a national civil rights group to advance justice and equity for black people in Britain created by some of the country's most influential black figures, it aims to dismantle systemic racism.

The group aims to focus on economic empowerment, bettering education, and health outcomes, combating racial discrimination and improving representation across society, as well as ensuring housing access and opportunities for black Britons across the country.

We have a problem in the UK, which apart from being wholly unfair, will set us back in business.

RACE IN THE UK WORKPLACE

Of course, not all racism and bias is covert. British cricketer Azeem Rafiq, who has South Asian heritage and is Muslim, testified through harrowing accounts at his employment tribunal with Yorkshire Cricket Club. Rafiq spoke about being physically pinned down and having red wine poured down his throat at age 15 when as Muslim the holy Qur'an describes different categories of foods, and alcohol falls under the category which is prohibited because it is harmful to the body, and that which is harmful to the body is harmful to the spirit, so this was a huge violation in addition being called racist slurs and much more. The Business in the Community 2021 Race at Work survey which captures the views of over 24,600 employees in the UK, found that global majority employees are twice as likely than white employees to have experienced or witnessed racist harassment from managers, customers, clients, and colleagues.

The report also found that six in ten white employees say that they feel they have an equal opportunity in the workplace, compared to five in ten from the global majority. In June 2021, Henley Business School published The Equity Effect report, which highlighted some data that contrasted with the government's view:

- One in three business leaders acknowledge racial inequity exists in their business.

- Two in five employees from the global majority acknowledge racial inequity exists in workplaces.

However, where perhaps there was some alignment with the government's view was that *Business leaders rated achieving racial equity as the least important challenge to overcome in the next 12 months.*

One of the most pertinent findings from the Henley research was that businesses which took practical steps towards achieving genuine equity recorded 58% higher revenue than those who did not. Showing a correlation between businesses which commit to investing in their people and financial performance.

The business case for racial equity is clear, but the prioritising is not.

In addition, you'll see on websites of large companies across the UK public targets but that don't always have a clear roadmap on how to achieve them as it has never been done before.

Equity is truly the capstone of the journey through diversity, inclusion, and equality, achieving equity creates a sense of community and engagement as well as positively impacting bottom lines.

Key Facts[8]

- Race equality in the UK will potentially bring a £24 billion per year boost to the UK economy – 1.3% gross domestic product. That is, £481 million a week.

- Organisations with more diverse teams have 36% better financial returns.

- Only 1 in 16 people at senior levels in the private and public sectors is from the global majority.

- The number of organisations voluntarily capturing their ethnicity pay gap data has increased from 11% in 2018 to 19% in 2021.

- The number of senior leaders as executive sponsors at the top table promoting equality, equity, fairness, and inclusion has increased from 32% in 2015 and 33% in 2018 to 44% in 2021.

- However, access to mentorship and sponsorship has reduced for people from the global majority since 2018.

NOTES

1. November 2021 CIPD conference.

2. *Racial Equity Tools website* https://www.racialequitytools.org/about.

3. Bhavnani, R., Mirza, H. S., & V. Meetoo, V. (2005, November 8). *Tackling the roots of racism: Lessons for success*. The Policy Press.

4. *Sources*: Pew Research Centre, Public Health England, Office for National Statistics, and Equality and Human Rights Commission.

5. Williams, W. (2020, March). *Windrush lessons learned review*. Home Office.

6. ONS. (2019). Updating ethnic contrasts in deaths involving the coronavirus (COVID-19), England, 24 January 2020 to 31 March 2021.

7. https://blackequityorg.com/manifesto/

8. BITC's race at work 2021 scorecard report produced in partnership with YouGov.

Chapter Two

DEEPENING OUR KNOWLEDGE
OF LIVED EXPERIENCE

Storytelling is essential to bring to life the lived experience of those from the global majority, otherwise those narratives will be buried and untold and as a result nothing changes. By listening to someone's story you can experience an alternative truth to your own, neither will be right or wrong but we can learn from the two truths sitting side by side. However, asking those from the global majority to share their story repeatedly for your learning, is like asking someone to re-open a healed wound just so you can understand their pain, so ensure that they are willing, and you are learning from it.

In this chapter, I share Albert's story which is a combination of anecdotes shared with me repeatedly during my years developing those from the global majority. I challenge you to step into his shoes, absorb the learning, and gain deeper insight and knowledge into what you may have overlooked in the past.

ALBERT'S STORY

Albert is male and in his late 40s. He is 6 ft tall and has dark skin, he has a medium build. When Albert smiles, you can't help but smile too and when he booms out his loud laugh, it is contagious.

He grew up in a London suburb with his three sisters and parents. His dad came to England from the Caribbean in his teens and his mum has South Asian heritage and was born in the UK.

His mum worked at the local authority and worked her way up to a management position and his dad took jobs decorating and labouring when he could find work. Although his dad had tried hard to secure permanent work, he found that he was always the first to be laid off or blamed if there was a problem on the job. The family struggled financially when Albert was a child, although they were never short of practical love which looked like strict curfews, encouragement to do well at school, food on the table, and lots of chores. Eventually, Albert's parents were able to buy the home that they were renting from the council, which they were extremely proud of.

Albert found school a challenge not because he wasn't bright but because he was always ahead. His dad had bought him encyclopedias and Albert would read them cover to cover when he was little. The teacher didn't like that he was ahead of the class, and because he stood out being tall and dark skinned, compared to the majority of peers, he would also get the blame for being disruptive even if he wasn't. He would of course complain about the injustice, which only made things worse as the teachers began describing him as a child that 'was always challenging authority'. This exasperated his feelings of **otherness** which had started early, being told that he was 'poo coloured' in primary school. Being mistaken for sales assistants or catering staff rather than a customer or consumer when he was out with his friends.

Eventually he was moved into a class with those who had special educational needs, he became despondent and started playing truant and ended up excluded from mainstream school and educated in a pupil referral unit. During that time, he started to believe that he wasn't very bright and couldn't see a future for himself.

After leaving education, he felt lost for a while, doing nothing much and hanging around with those like himself who weren't in education, employment, or training. Although encouraged to get up to no good, his strict upbringing meant that he was more afraid of the wrath of his parents than the peer pressure of his friends. When strongly encouraged by the job centre, he tried sales jobs, labouring on construction sites, and eventually secured a job at a retailer part time. The retailer valued how quickly he picked things up and how good he was with people and encouraged him to go full time and consider working his way up the ladder.

His family were proud of him, they were so pleased that he could turn his life around. His dad would give him advice to 'play the game' and not stand out, whatever he should do, 'don't let your guard down', remember that these people (his colleagues) are not your friends. His dad counselled him to not challenge their behaviour, or he would be dismissed, as had happened to him many times.

Things were going well for Albert, yes, he experienced the odd comment. 'I don't see colour, it doesn't matter if you're red, green, yellow, or blue, you're one of us' and being mistaken for the only other colleague from the global majority, even by people who he'd worked with for years, when they looked nothing like each other. He'd learned to take a deep breath and temper what he said, as whenever he was as passionate as his colleagues, they're reaction would be that they appeared afraid of him.

He found himself jumping through more hoops than his colleagues too, they kept dangling the opportunity of promotion at him, but he always had to do one more thing to prove himself, and it was often taking on the roles that no one else would do. At first, he enjoyed the challenge but was now becoming tired of it.

At one point there was a theft in the business, and it really felt like they were trying to blame him. Albert had a lot of sleepless nights because of it. Luckily someone came forward who knew who the thief was, but if they hadn't Albert felt that he would have been sacked without any evidence, or a second chance.

The final straw came when he went for promotion for the third time and was told that there was really nothing between him and the other candidate, but they felt that the other candidate was just the 'right fit', even though Albert's track record and experience far outweighed the other candidate.

Albert had a mentor at work, and sought their opinion 'do you think my ethnicity could be hampering my career progression?' he asked. The mentor squirmed uncomfortably on their seat and said that they were sure that it was nothing to do with anything like that and encouraged him to look to the positive and work on how he can improve his gravitas and confidence.

Albert has now become demotivated at work. His line manager seems like a nice enough person, he doesn't do anything wrong but neither does he go out of his way to help him. He has told Albert about a course that he can attend to help him move up the ladder designed especially for those from the global majority, but Albert feels that it is a **tokenistic** gesture and doesn't believe that it will make any difference. His performance ratings are dropping, and he is now being performance managed. To top it off his mum is unwell, and he wants to take an active role in caring for her.

Although he has now been with the company for seven years, he intends to resign next week. He has just had enough.

ALBERT'S MANAGER

Albert's manager, Richard, is in his late 40s, always jolly and smiling. His mum is from Wales and his dad is from England, and he grew up in East London, with his older sister. His dad worked in a warehouse and his mum was a secretary when he was growing up, not lots of money but lots of love. He was an average student, not the best or the worse, he secured an apprenticeship and fell in love with retail and has been working his way up the ladder and has done quite well for himself, now in a senior manager role.

Richard has started to become more interested in diversity, equity, and inclusion, his CEO is really committed, and the enthusiasm is infectious, he is hearing a lot about it at work and feels that it very much aligned with how he lives his life. His close network is mostly white and English, but his son had married a girl with Chinese heritage, and they'd welcomed her into the family. However, he did remember his sister once bringing a Black boy home and his dad not being too happy about it, she never brought him round again. He also never had any close friends from the global majority growing up and the depictions of people from the global majority in the media when he was growing up, he acknowledged, were minimal and generally negative.

Lately, Richard has been feeling torn, he wants to treat all of his colleagues the same. Fairness is at the heart of who he is, and he feels that everyone should have the same opportunity. After all he didn't grow up in a privileged environment but through hard work and a couple of lucky breaks he got where he is today. He sees Albert's career slipping away, in fact he realises that this is a trend with him and in the business generally, he hasn't known what to do the last few times that he's recruited colleagues from the global majority and after what seemed like a promising start their enthusiasm had dissipated. He really wanted this time to be different.

At first, he rationalised that his previous recruits just weren't the right fit for the business, but now he was starting to question if it was something that he'd been doing as a leader. Some unconscious bias maybe?

He has overheard some of the banter between Albert and his colleagues, some of it he would class as a bit close to the bone, but he didn't want to step in, in case he seemed overbearing or embarrassed Albert. He asked Albert if he was OK, and he said that he was fine. He'd tell him if he wasn't, wouldn't he? His door was always open, and he was always happy to see Albert, they didn't necessarily have the same conversations as he had with some of the other colleagues who supported the same football team and liked to go running. He felt that Albert was a bit more formal and less relaxed and although always professional some of that informal chat that builds a deeper relationship just didn't happen between them.

As Richard reflected on:

- whether he was being curious enough and listening, and willing to step into Albert shoes;

- how willing he was to show some vulnerability and admit that he didn't know what to do to help realise Albert's potential; and

- whether he was being the ambassador for change and ally that he wanted to be, or whether he is being a passive bystander?

An email pinged into his mailbox; it was from Albert requesting a meeting outside of their usual one to one cycle. He feared that Albert wanted to hand in his resignation.

Reflecting on Albert's Story

Before I go on to help you take an equity lens on Albert's story, I encourage you to take a moment to reflect on your own, with your team or with a group of peers. Here are some prompts for you:

- Is it possible that a similar story to Albert or Richard could be told by someone in your organisation?
- What could Richard or an HR person have done to intervene before this point?
- What might equity look like for Albert?
- What resistance do you have to the story? Why is that?

THE SYSTEM

I want to start by acknowledging that **systemic racism** exists, this is the notion that a form of racism is embedded in the laws and regulations of a society or an organisation. It manifests as discrimination in areas such as criminal justice, employment, housing, health care, education, and political representation.

Systemic racism shows up in Albert's story in his education. Even now exclusion rates are five times higher for Black Caribbean pupils in parts of England according to the government website. Exclusion rates for mixed-race students with one parent who is white and one parent who had Black Caribbean heritage were more than four times higher than their white peers in several local authorities.[1] A recent report by the Institute of Race Relations (IRR) warned of a 'PRU [pupil referral unit] to prison' pipeline for working-class Black children.[2]

WHY WAS ALBERT'S INTELLIGENCE SEEN AS A PROBLEM?

It can be argued that the school system in the UK is institutionally racist with unfair policies and practices, discriminatory treatment, and inequitable opportunities and outcomes. A school system that concentrates those from the global majority in the most over-crowded and underresourced schools with the least qualified teachers compared to the educational opportunities of white students is an example of institutional racism.

Although the **adultification** of Black children is a symptom of the wider systemic problem, it is worth understanding to make sense of Albert's experience.

Being described as 'streetwise' or 'aggressive', or for girls being more likely to be seen as 'hyper sexualised', the impact is that they can't be vulnerable and are not as protected. Albert's behaviour was misinterpreted at school, instead of giving him more stretching work to do and recognising that he was bored, he was instead labelled a difficult child.

EMPLOYMENT

Now let's looks at employment. Albert's mum was employed, but his dad struggled and indeed Albert found it difficult to get his foot on the career ladder. This plays out when we look at the UK unemployment rate which was 4.0% in October–December 2021. The rate was 3.5% for people from a white ethnic background compared to 7.7% for people from the global majority, although there was substantial variation among the global majority. People from white (3.5%) and Indian (4.4%) ethnic backgrounds had the lowest unemployment rates, and people from Pakistani (10.2%) and Bangladeshi (9.4%) ethnic backgrounds had the highest rates in October–December 2021.

Albert had a role model who worked but his dad in particular had challenges keeping a job and so didn't have networks or advice on how to successfully navigate the workplace, and although his mum could provide some support, she did not know what it was like to navigate the workplace as a Black man.

MICROAGGRESSIONS

Microaggressions are statements, actions, or incidents regarded as an instance of indirect, subtle, or unintentional discrimination against members of a marginalised group such as those from the global majority. Comments like 'I don't see colour, it doesn't matter if you're red, green, yellow, or blue, you're one of us' are usually well intentioned, but thinking back to the seesaw, equal sandbags provide unequal outcomes, and to not see colour is to deny difference exists and when we deny that a difference exists it gives us permission to ignore racism and disengage from conversations on equity. Being mistaken for the only other colleague from the global majority is an all too common form of microaggression that people from the global majority experience in the workplace. Dismissing the racialised experiences of those from the global majority is oppressive and continues to give weight only to the white experience. Along with that, colourblind thinking dismisses the reality of racial privilege and as a result nothing changes.

Njeri Mathis Rutledge,[3] a Black female law professor describes walking a tightrope in the work environment:

I deal with racism constantly. I walk a daily tightrope where I must appear as though all is well despite the barrage of images of unarmed Blacks being killed, racist attacks, and the growth of **white supremacy**. *Even the legal academy fails to provide a haven from racist attitudes.*

I believe that Albert would relate to this, walking the tightrope of acceptable behaviours, knowing that one step too far to the left or the right, could have a significant negative impact on his career.

Microaggressions – The Four Ds	
The *d*ouble takes	Two colleagues walk into a meeting, and it is automatically assumed that the white colleague is more senior, and the colleague from the global majority must correct them.
	'Are you sure that you are meant to be in this meeting, it's for x grade and above, you couldn't possibly be senior enough'
	To always be questioned and then question yourself about whether you should be there, leads to constant second guessing which can tie you up in knots.

Microaggressions – The Four Ds	
The doubting of your competency	Questioning where your education took place as your level of intelligence surpasses their biased expectation of someone from the global majority. 'You're really intelligent aren't you, what university did you attend, you're so articulate?'
	Indicating that they don't want to take your word for it, even though you are the expert in the room, with a comment like 'Is there someone more senior that we can check that with?'
The dismissals of your experience	'I don't think that they meant to exclude you, ignore you, undermine you ...'
	'I don't see colour, so anything relating to race is not valid in our conversations'
The domain you find yourself within	Albert going for a job interview and seeing that all previous post holders had been white men via photos on the wall, tells him indirectly that his face is unlikely to fit.

These microaggressions can also breed and feed imposter syndrome[4]

Physical aggressions would be treated very differently, however small, imagine if you saw your colleague being prodded in the ribs each day with a pencil by numerous people, would you step in? The power imbalance makes microaggressions so dangerous, if the aggressor has more power and racial privilege, then the person from the global majority can't speak up for fear of the consequences.

To create racial justice in the workplace is to recognise pain and injustice and to care about it. If you treat people as humans, you can't pretend that your colleagues aren't suffering. It takes personal bravery not to walk past but to get involved, not to be a **passive bystander**. It takes an openness to admit that you are wrong when you inevitably make mistakes. And even more to agitate the system or organisational culture. It is lifelong work, just like learning is lifelong too.

It takes curiosity, wonder, and open eyes to learn about the lives of others to see through their eyes is to see the world anew. Imagine a world where justice was assured, do you want to repeat the mistakes already made or transform to more equitable workplaces?

Non-verbal Bias

Notice your body language, the shift of your body away from someone when they speak. Gesturing in someone's direction when you are speaking about a stereotype, for example, 'our Hispanic colleagues have this problem...'

These actions betray your unconscious thoughts and those from the global majority see it, feel it, and are impacted by it. It may be unconscious and unintentional but that doesn't make it OK. It is important for you to be vulnerable, ask for feedback on your body language in order to make the unconscious conscious and change it.

RACE VS CLASS

As I interviewed senior diversity, equity, and inclusion leads in the public, private, and third sector for my research for this book, a number of those I spoke to mentioned social class and talked about solving the class divide as the panacea of inequity. As anyone from the global majority in the UK knows, unfortunately resolving class does not solve racial issues.

In August 2020, Dawn Butler MP a Black woman was stopped by the police while driving to Sunday lunch with a friend and felt that they had been **racially profiled**. There was no other reason that she could explain for being stopped. Other Members of Parliament from the global majority have shared similar experiences. The government statistics in October 2020 found that Black people were nine times more likely to be stopped and searched by police officers than white people in the UK. Class does not help you avoid this fact, neither does it stop you being socially profiled while shopping; in 2013, billionaire, US media mogul, Oprah Winfrey reported that she was the victim of racism on a trip to Switzerland when a shop assistant refused to show her a handbag because it was 'too expensive'. This shows that even a person worth billions can't escape racial profiling.

Those who have achieved senior roles at work from the global majority can feel insecure in their position, they may not have generational wealth and support to fall back on, and may be the first in the family to achieve these positions. They may feel that their position is tenuous due to self-sabotaging thoughts, lack of support by others, and being ill-equipped to be successful in this space. Albert's working-class up bringing may not have prepared him for the upper echelons of the business world, and the intersection of his race and class may have a compound effect of disadvantage.

The pioneering scholar and writer,[5] Kimberle Crenshaw describes **intersectionality** as a lens, a prism, for seeing the way in which various forms of inequality often operate together and exacerbate each other. We tend to talk about race inequality as separate from inequality based on gender, class, sexuality, or immigrant status, but they intersect. The Centre for Intersectional Justice describes intersectionality as about fighting discrimination within discrimination, tackling inequalities within inequalities, and protecting minorities within minorities. Although it has been documented that white working-class boys particularly those who qualify for free school meals are being left behind in the system, it's class that holds them back not ethnicity and class, and the compound effect of discrimination that creates.

ETHNICITY PAY GAP

The **ethnicity pay gap,** meaning the difference between the median hourly earnings of all from the global majority (not including white minority) groups and white groups, is at its lowest level since 2012 at 2.3%. Employees from the white Irish, Indian, and Chinese ethnic groups on average have higher hourly earnings than the white British ethnic group according to government statistics.

Those from the global majority have been making progress up the professional and occupational class ladders, though some more than others, and there remains underrepresentation at the very top. Employees from the global majority are more likely than those from a white British background to say that experiencing discrimination contributed to their failure in achieving their career expectations (20% vs 11%).

Also, using data from previous reviews led by Baroness Ruby McGregor-Smith and Sir John Parker, evidence heard from a wide range of stakeholders, and an examination of new data, the Commission identified four areas of focus, including **ethnicity pay gap** data reporting.

The executive recruitment agency Green Park's Colour of Power project has recently found that 52 out of 1,099 of the 'most powerful jobs' in the UK were held by those from the global majority. That is 4.7%. It concluded that Britain's leadership positions had failed to improve between 2017 and 2020, with only 15 additional global majority-held roles since 2017.

When looking at the top of the FTSE 100, we see that there has been an improvement in the representation of those from the global majority on Boards just in this last year. In January 2020, 52 FTSE 100 companies had ethnic representation on their boards, and in November 2020 this figure rose to 74. However, at the same time, the number of Black people at the very top of the top FTSE 100 companies (meaning chair, chief executive, or chief financial officer) recently fell from 2 to 0 (reported in February 2021).

The top of UK business and academia remain notably white while the public sector in general has a better track record than the private.

Losing out on promotions like Albert has done, will have kept his salary low, possibly while watching his peers surpass him, and even at the grade he is at, it's highly likely that he could be being paid less than his white counterparts due to the ethnicity pay gap.

ACCENT BIAS

One of the big challenges for those in the global majority can be their voice or accent. If they were not born in the UK, the different rhythms and sounds of their native tongue, even though they are speaking English, may get in the way of them being understood or taken seriously at times. If their voice doesn't match how they are expected to sound this can also cause an issue.

A study sample[6] of over a thousand members of the public were asked to listen to and evaluate mock interview answers spoken in five different accents, including Received Pronunciation (which is the standard form of British English pronunciation, based on educated speech in southern England, widely accepted as a standard elsewhere), Estuary English, Multicultural London English, General Northern English, and Urban West Yorkshire English. The research was aimed at understanding the impact a person's accent has on their work opportunities and life outcomes.

We all have automatic associations with voices. Bias becomes discrimination when we allow these associations to govern our judgement of unrelated traits such as intelligence or competence. This does feel extremely unfair, especially as further research has shown that those with non-standard accents face disadvantages in pay, and are less likely to be promoted to middle and senior leadership.

Recruitment managers overwhelmingly rated those who didn't speak with Received Pronunciation (the standard form of British English pronunciation, based on educated speech in southern England) as least influential, least likely to be a team player, least innovative, and so least qualifying for upper management. And further research from the London School of Economics into non-native accents and managerial positions found a perception that those who are non-native speakers, or those who have an accent, will have less political skill than others. Political skill is crucial for senior roles, where influencing and leading are critical.

CULTURAL INTELLIGENCE

Western cultures tend to be youth-centric, emphasising attributes like individualism and independence. This relates back to the Protestant work ethic, which ties an individual's value to their ability to work, which diminishes in old age. As their health deteriorates, the elderly in these cultures often move to retirement communities, assisted living facilities, and nursing homes. Whereas in many global majority communities, elders act as the head of the household. The elders are supported by the younger members of the family and they in turn play a key role in raising their grandchildren. As a result, there can be a duty and desire to look after elderly parents, something that might not be appreciated by Albert's manager if he doesn't have that cultural intelligence. That lack of tuning in and appreciating of cultural difference can mean the difference between retaining and losing key colleagues.

TOP TIPS – ADVANCING RACIAL EQUITY

(1) Share something that is not obvious about your background just by looking at you and see if this begins a two-way dialogue.

(2) Reflect on obstacles and challenges that your colleagues from the global majority may have experienced and may still be experiencing and work together to remove barriers and obstacles. Don't assume.

(3) Increase your awareness of biases[7] that you hold, such as **affinity bias**, recruiting in your image; **prove it again bias**, asking your global majority colleagues to prove themselves over and above what you would ask of their white counterparts and **tightrope bias**, where only a very narrow set of behaviours are accepted from them and then take actions to overcome them. For example, in a meeting about promotions, you could call out if you believe that prove it again bias is at play and advocate for that colleague's promotion.

(4) When re-structuring or making layoffs, ensure that those from the global majority are not disproportionately impacted.

(5) Educate others on what microaggressions are and create environments that do not tolerate them.

(6) Recognise that an intersectional approach is key, but that doesn't mean that you do not talk about race and ethnicity.

(7) Look at your ethnicity pay gap data, be transparent about the findings, and plan to close the gap.

(8) Develop yours and your colleague's cultural intelligence, the capability to adapt and interact effectively with others from different cultures.

(9) Appreciate that talent doesn't just look and behave in one way. To do so, separate performance from potential and personality from skill sets.

NOTES

1. https://www.ethnicity-facts-figures.service.gov.uk/education-skills-and-training/absence-and-exclusions/permanent-exclusions/latest

2. The IRR's new paper, *How Black Working-Class Youth are Criminalised and Excluded in the English School System: A London Case Study.*

3. Rutledge, N. M. (2021). Walking the tightrope: Reflections of a Black female law professor. *Campbell Law Review, 43,* 233.

4. Clance, P., & Imes, S. (1978). Imposter phenomenon. A psychological phenomenon which leads you to feel like a fraud and that you don't measure up.

5. Crenshaw, K. (1991, July). Mapping the margins: Intersectionality, identity politics, and violence against women of color. *Stanford Law Review, 43*(6), 1241–1299.

6. Accent Bias Britain Research – February 2020.

7. Williams, J. C., & Mihaylo, S. (2019, December). How the best bosses interrupt bias on their teams.

Chapter Three

BEING AN EMPATHETIC CHANGEMAKER

It is not our differences that divides us. It is our inability to recognise, accept, and celebrate those differences.
(Audre Lorde)

What does it take to make change happen around racial inequity? What type of leader do you need to be and what qualities do you need to develop? The qualities of leaders evolve with each generation depending on what we face. We are in a time of rapid change where we need to be adaptive. COVID-19, the evolving of technology, *Roe* v *Wade*[1] being overturned, and Brexit tell us that major change is possible, and not always in the direction we wish, so we must have our voices heard.

Leadership is at the centre of this change. It's important to develop your level of empathy, not sympathy, if you want to help move your organisation from equality to equity. Sympathy involves understanding from your own perspective. Empathy involves putting yourself in the other person's shoes and understanding why they may have these feelings.

Being an empathetic changemaker is what it takes to drive change, this is not about being a caretaker or a safe pair of hands and accepting the status quo, it's about shaking things up with a large dose of courage and compassion. It is about moving from being a good person who doesn't act, to one who does.

This is a calling to be the best version of yourself in service of racial equity in the workplace and the ripple effect that will have in society.

Here's what it takes and how you can achieve it.

SEEK ALTERNATIVE TRUTHS

It can be confronting when someone shares a truth that is conflicting with your own, but if we make a practice of always seeking out these alternative truths, we can be more embracing of different perspectives, views, and lived experience. For example, two people attend the same meeting, one leaves saying that it was a productive and egalitarian meeting in which everyone participated and had air time, the other leaves feeling dismissed, feeling unheard, and that nothing was achieved, both can be correct simultaneously. Always asking 'what if' is a way of cultivating this approach in you and your colleagues. Do go beyond asking the question and explore this alternative truth in as much detail as you can, it may lead to a breakthrough for you.

- What if this was easy?
- What if we could listen to the message, not the accent in which it was delivered?
- What if our colleagues didn't have to **cover** parts of their identity to be successful at work?
- What if we could comfortably talk about race and ethnicity?
- What if we were all open to listening and adapting?
- What if we committed to our next five hires being those from the global majority?
- What if there wasn't really scarcity of roles, but different turns, opportunities, and ways of working?
- What if we were brave?
- What if they are the right fit for the role, and we can shape the role to fit them?

The Case of the Folding Bike

Pooja recently bought a folding bike, a great way to get some exercise and look after the environment at the same time. She rides it to work, folds it up in the foyer and stores it in a cupboard. She has a colleague who has been doing this for years, but on the third day of riding her bike in, she was called into an office and told it was breaching company guidance. She checked with her white male colleague whether he had been spoken to, and no one had said anything to him. She realised that being a person from the global majority at work made her hyper visible and an easy target for unfairness. The rules existed for everyone, but were more rigorously applied to her.

What if you were aware of your own double standards?

RADICAL HUMBLING

The reverberations of someone from the global majority reaching the C-Suite are so vast – for their community, future generations of their family and the world. (Senior DEI Leader)

This is about sharing power, remember the seesaw. To balance we may need to give something up. You first need to acknowledge that you have power and then decide to share it and normalise sharing power rather than evangelise about how unique you are in doing it. This behaviour should not be rare but commonplace, like saying 'thank you', when you are served in a cafe.

A study by Catalyst[2] found that humility is one of the four critical leadership factors for creating an environment where employees from different demographic backgrounds feel included.

A definition of humility that makes sense to me is: *Humility is the acceptance of your own flaws and shortcomings.* I believe that all leaders should do this.

Radical humbling looks like:

- Not feeling frustrated that you don't know what's being said in **Employee Resource Groups**. Some spaces are not for you and that's not personal because, it's about **psychological safety** for those in the room.

- Being open to being in the wrong and not fully understanding. Just like men cannot know what it's like to be pregnant or give birth, however many times they watch movies, listen to stories, or even witness it live. Sometimes you just don't have the lived experience, so you may never fully understand, and as a result you may make mistakes.

- Share your feelings of vulnerability and resistance. If you're terrified of getting it wrong, it's OK to say that.

- Humility requires you to really listen to feedback and accept that you have prejudices, flaws, and shortcomings, which you are willing to work on.

Psychological Safety for All

Be aware of the lack of safety that your white colleagues can also experience, some have shared that they can feel like there is a target on their back and language like 'pale, male and stale' will offend. And that when they have spoken up on behalf of their colleagues from the global majority, their fellow white colleagues have alienated them.

Humility may come naturally to you, but if it doesn't try the following three approaches:

(1) *Ask for feedback*. Humility involves an accurate view of your-self. Have you asked for feedback in the last seven days? Ask trusted colleagues to be honest about what you do well when it comes to racial equity and where you can develop. You can be proud of your strengths, while working on your development areas. Without feedback, it is impossible to judge if what you are doing is working for you and for others, find

your blind spots and own your communications. When you have the feedback, you must be seen to act on it.

(2) *Confront your prejudices.* Humility is about having an open mind, but you will have prejudices and biases. So, you have to think about how you can challenge your prejudices, you could firstly become more aware of them, using something like the **Implicit Association Test** and then work on them. For example, if you found that you had a bias against people with a particular ethnic background, it would be good for you to intentionally spend time with people from that background to deepen the understanding and connection with them.

(3) *Start with a question.* If you think you already know everything or act like you do, others won't take the time to help you get educated in the complex world of racial equity and as a result your knowledge won't grow.

Really listen. You can ask many questions, but if you don't listen to the responses, it will be a waste of time. Listening does not mean that you agree, but it does help dial down your own pride. Yours is not the only way of thinking or doing. After someone shares an opinion or experience, take a moment to digest what they have said before you speak.

Lastly in your quest for radical humility, you must accept setbacks. We've all been humbled by our own or other's experiences, haven't we, when we realise that we are not infallible. Humility allows you to accept challenges without the fear of failure. And when those failures inevitably come, you can use it as a learning experience to do it better next time. Be careful not to mistake insecurity and inadequacy for humility. Humility has nothing to do with the insecure and inadequate. Just like arrogance has nothing to do with greatness!

ACCOUNTABILITY

By accountability, I don't mean football manager style, one bad match and you are sacked. I mean supported, encouraged, and held to deliver on promises. Little is learned from being sacked or 'cancelled' every time we don't deliver. We can learn so much more from persevering and delivering on our promises.

Think about your current leader. Are they personally account-able? Do they instil accountability in you? How do you role model accountability?

Would people say that you take personal accountability? If so, are you as good at keeping your promises to yourself as you are to others? Accountability looks like publicly and sincerely apologising when you get it wrong and talking about the steps you are going to take to put things right. Accountability looks like acknowledging that there is a problem in your team, department, organisation, or society and you owning your part in that problem and the solution.

PERSEVERANCE

If we look throughout the world in every industry, in every culture, there's one consistent trend among successful changemakers, and that trend is the ability to persevere. It's the ability to stand up and take a step forward when everyone else sits down.

You can build your perseverance muscle by:

- *Desire.* You have to really want to achieve racial equity, some-times we don't want something enough to do the hard work or persevere sufficiently to obtain it. What are you willing to stop doing, what effort are you willing to invest?

- *Self-belief.* You must truly believe that you have the qualities and skills to achieve your preferred outcome, or that you can acquire them. Limiting beliefs, like 'what if I get it wrong' or, 'what if I am labelled a racist', will undermine your ability to persevere and absorb some of the energy that you want to use to power towards your goals.

- *Definiteness of plans.* Goal setting is a key aspect of persever-ing. If you don't know where you are going, how can you get there? Even if your plans aren't perfect, you should have some-thing that you are loosely aiming for, it provides focus and a level of accountability needed to persevere. If your plans are vague and undefined, your levels of perseverance will dwindle.

- *Willpower.* When navigating the new territory of racial equity, the capacity to override an unwanted thought, feeling,

or impulse to keep cool and calm under pressure and to
consciously self-regulate all require will power.

- *Habit.* Persistence is the direct result of habit. Our mind
  absorbs what we feed it. If we repeat acts of courage, we
  will overcome our fears. Perhaps you are nervous about
  asking others about their culture and background, you could
  set a regular weekly activity where one person brings in an
  item to talk about in order to share their culture, heritage,
  and what's important to them. That habit could help you
  persevere against your fears. What do you need to start challenging yourself to do?

- *Focus.* It's important not to get distracted from this work, we
  all have competing commitments and addressing inequity can
  feel like the latest initiative in a long line, but this work must
  be embedded in the DNA of all that you do.

- *Set deadlines.* Many of us are pressure prompted, which means
  that we spring into action when we have little time left to
  achieve a task. If we don't have a deadline or the deadline is
  a long way off, we can find it difficult to start. So, I recommend that you break the task down into smaller tasks and set
  shorter-term deadlines that will provide the pressure that you
  need.

- *Measure and track.* There is a great saying 'what gets
  measured, gets done'. Measure your ethnicity pay gap, your
  recruitment and retention at all levels, use an intersectional
  lens, listen to what is and is not being said in exit interviews, and use anonymous colleague surveys and information from **listening circles** and **employee resource groups** to
  help you.

- *Agenda.* Set racial equity as an agenda item in every meeting that makes you stop and consider the equity within your
  discussions and decisions, until it becomes a habitual way
  of thinking. Ask, who is not in the room and what would
  they say if they were. Or how can you consult further to
  ensure that you are coming up with equitable solutions?

ACT WITH INTEGRITY

For the change to stick and create sustainable change, the change-maker must have integrity. In research on leadership, integrity is consistently rated as one of the most important character traits of a respected leader. Integrity can be defined as making values-based decisions, not decisions based on personal gain.

A way to assess your integrity is to ask yourself if you would behave in the same way if someone was watching you. If you were acting with integrity, you'd do the same thing whether or not you were being observed, because you'd believe that it was the right thing to do. Don't get me wrong, people with integrity aren't perfect, but they admit their mistakes and do what they can to right their wrongs.

When integrity is missing from our relationships, our leaders, or ourselves, a break down in trust occurs, and we know that without **psychological safety** progress stalls or regresses.

Aligning our internal values with our external behaviours sounds easy but putting it into practice can be a challenge.

Be a role model of integrity for others. Ensure that your morals and ethics align with your behaviour. Be consistent, open, and clear with your morals and ethics. Encourage those around you to question you and others, especially when you/they don't appear to be acting with integrity. For example, if a colleague proposes an approach that you think is questionable in regard to your ethics around inclusion, you could say 'Tell me about how what you just suggested fits in with our values around inclusion?' This approach is curious and collaborative rather than conflictual.

Stand up for what you believe in. You'll always feel better about yourself for standing up for what you believe in. You can do this in a respectful and positive way. Always ask 'How could I satisfy my ethics while also accommodating your outcomes?' Aim for a win–win, it is possible with some positive and creative thinking.

Keep your agreements. Keep your word to yourself and others. Every day we make promises, so many that it's easy to forget them and when we do forget them we jeopardise our relationships. Every small broken promise erodes trust. If you make a commitment, write it down and only cross it off once it's done, or let the person know if you can no longer fulfil it.

Surround yourself with people of integrity. Limit time spent with those who don't hold your values and ethics and if you are in a position to recruit people, consider how you hire people that have similar morals and ethics to you, while not using it as an excuse to reinforce biased recruiting.

CHANNEL ANGER

You can have a myriad of emotions when you are awoken to the inequity in your workplace, and one of them can be anger. Anger about inequality, mistreatment, and injustice can be channelled for good. Anger can spur an entire culture to change for the better, as witnessed by the civil rights movement of the 1960s.

Next time don't just rant or simmer in the corner, do something. Mobilise your rage into something positive; something that makes a difference. The odds are that there are lots of people just as angry as you.

AWARENESS AND ACTION ARE AT THE HEART OF CHANGE

For the empathetic changemaker, it all starts with increasing your awareness of your unconscious and conscious associations:

When you think of women workers do you think mum?

Do you associate part-time workers with lack of commitment to the role or organisation?

Do you assume that your colleague with East Asian heritage is highly intelligent and great at maths?

Our associations are automatic, a little like reaching for another biscuit from the packet to accompany our tea, but we don't need to surrender to it. We learn to discipline ourselves to recognise what is bad for us and change our behaviour. That same journey is the one we need to take to make our workplaces better.

Something to look out for to increase your awareness, is your 'Yes Buts':

- Yes but, what about the white working-class boys.

- Yes but, this goes against everything I stand for, I believe in treating everyone the same.

- Yes but, I am already a good person, it's them not me.

Be aware of discomfort that you may experience while pushing change in yourself and others.
Be aware of the level of compassion needed for others and yourself on this journey to racial equity.

TIPS ON BEING AN EMPATHETIC CHANGEMAKER

- Know yourself, work on increasing your self awareness.

- Find those who disagree with you and listen to them – remember that there are alternative truths that can be equally correct.

- Own your power and use it to balance the seesaw – when you are radically humble, you use your power positively with humility.

- Explain 'Why' equity matters to you.

- Publicly commit to being a changemaker, and be held to account and do the same for others.

- Remain honest and transparent, especially when it's not good news. Align your actions with your values and embody integrity.

- Develop the resilience to persevere when you fall short or make mistakes.

- Don't get distracted, this is important work – a consistent focus is needed.

- Take action.

NOTES

1. *Roe v. Wade*, the landmark 1973 Supreme Court case that made abortion legal across the USA for the past five decades, has been overturned, and abortion is no longer protected at the federal level as of 24 June 2022. Instead, individual states will decide whether abortion is legal within their state boundaries.

2. Prime, J., & Salib, E. R. (2014). *Inclusive leadership: The view from six countries*. Catalyst.

Chapter Four

DEFINING OUR PATHWAYS TO ACTION

Injustice anywhere is a threat to justice everywhere. We are caught in an inescapable network of mutuality, tied in a single garment of destiny. Whatever affects one directly, affects all indirectly. (Martin Luther King, Jr, 'Letter from Birmingham Jail')

In this chapter, I provide some tangible steps that you can take towards achieving racial equity at work. These pathways to action were garnered from interviews with senior diversity, equity and inclusion leaders working in the public, private, and third sectors mainly based in the UK, some working globally, combined with the latest research, best practice, and my expertise working in the field of leadership, talent, and personal development.

There is not just one pathway to taking action, but these steps will guide you to create your own route map tailored to you and your organisation.

To create this route map you should:

(1) Ascertain collective knowledge.
(2) Bring to light your blind spots.
(3) Learn from your colleagues.
(4) Experiment to find what works for your context.

ASCERTAIN COLLECTIVE KNOWLEDGE

Ultimately you need to understand your current culture. It takes individual action to drive the collective action, and collective action springs from collective knowledge. You need to know what you know, and how you do what you do in your workplace, the formal and informal systems and behaviours, and values which create an experience for your colleagues and customers. Maybe your culture is one of the political gameplaying, or where if a senior manager decides that you are talented you rise up the ranks rapidly, or perhaps it's the hours that you put in that matter. Whatever the culture, everyone will know how things are done around here and it's worth spending some time to be clear on your current reality.

Gathering data is an important part of gaining collective knowledge, but it can be challenging. The Data Protection Act 2018 means that every organisation in the UK must follow 'data protection principles' and must make sure that data are used fairly, lawfully, and transparently.

You may have frustrations regarding limitations around collecting data, or the reticence of colleagues to declare their information, but there will be information that is available even if it isn't centralised or complete at this point. There will be information regarding your track record and future plans around racial inequity that is common knowledge to all in your organisation and maybe even externally. Work with what you have while continuing to encourage those who haven't declared their protected characteristics, such as gender, ethnicity, etc. to do so. Providing opportunities to disclose on an ongoing basis can help, as you may have more people disclosing their ethnicity during black history month if you run a significant and positive campaign. Or if you have a companywide launch of an equity, diversity, and inclusion strategy, that would also be a good a time, as would the recruitment and exit stage. Your colleagues will want to know why their data is being collected and what you will do with it, and this should be clear and transparent. If they have any fear that this data may be used against them, they will not disclose.

Examples of Collective Knowledge That You Can Ascertain

- Data and reports – climate surveys, annual reports, externally commissioned investigations, research, company statements, published targets, retention, performance matrix, and **ethnicity pay gap** data.

- Diagnostics such as cultural intelligence reports, extent to which colleagues are **covering**, and audits by external companies.

- Employee reviews of what it's like to work at your company hosted on external websites, such as Glassdoor.

- Employee resource groups – a powerful source of knowledge due to the safe space they provide, these groups may be willing to share high-level recurring themes from their discussions with you.

- Listening groups – when you have brought together colleagues from the global majority to share the challenges that they face in the workplace, this can be within a focus group type approach or you could use a fishbowl style, where those from the global majority speak and others silently observe. You may have run these internally or had an external provider facilitate and report on what emerged.

- Social media – what is being said by employees, customers, suppliers, and competitors about you and what you say about yourselves.

- Anecdotal and observed trends – analysing who progresses and who doesn't; who has their probation extended; and which candidates always come a close second in job interviews or for promotions. When you look at performance ratings, who is not performing well and why. How complaints regarding race and ethnicity are dealt with? How microaggressions or outright racism

is tackled and whose acting up opportunities and stretch
assignments are not reflected in their remuneration?

If the following areas aren't addressed in your climate or colleague surveys, you should consider doing so:

- How safe colleagues feel to talk about race and ethnicity
  at work.

- How equipped colleagues feel to talk about race and
  ethnicity at work.

This is not an exhaustive list of how you can ascertain collective
knowledge. Once you start to look, you'll find a wealth of data on
which to springboard your equity efforts, and at the very least gain
clarity about the gaps that need to be filled.

BRING TO LIGHT YOUR BLIND SPOTS

*Every age has its massive moral blind spots. We might not
see them, but our children will. (Bono)*

To reveal our organisational blind spots, we need to be vulnerable,
open to hearing feedback that might surprise or challenge how we
view ourselves and feel safe to make mistakes in the knowledge
that there will not be repercussions. Most importantly, we must
take action from the feedback we receive, otherwise we set relationships and progress backwards.

Some Places to Look for Potential Blind Spots

- You may not realise the blind spots in your decision
  making. Perhaps, only those from certain educational
  backgrounds are being recognised as talent in your
  organisation. A recent example experienced in the UK was

the Tory party election following the resignation of Boris
Johnson. On paper the candidate pool looked like the
most ethnically diverse ever, however, all were university
educated and most attended private school. This sent the
message that as long as your lived experience is like mine,
you speak my language with the same accent, frequent the
same places, only then are you considered to be someone
who I can share my power with. In other words, you can
be a person from the global majority and be successful
only if you assimilate.

- Colleagues not feeling that they can be themselves at work
  and so **covering** to fit in – for example, colleagues feeling
  that they can't wear their hijab at work for fear of discrimination and stereotyping, so instead they assimilate by
  taking it off for work, even though it's important to them.

- Conversations and offhand comments often reveal blind
  spots and **gaslighting**. An example of gaslighting is when a
  colleague from the global majority is told that they only got
  the job to tick a box, which is hugely undermining, or when
  someone from the global majority makes a complaint, and
  are made to feel that it's probably their fault. For example,
  saying something like 'Are you sure that you are experiencing microaggressions, maybe you just have different person-
  alities, or you are being too sensitive?'

- Policies created without a diverse group of people in the
  room will always have blind spots. Look at what you are
  saying and what you are not saying – For example, if you
  don't mention men with dreadlocks when your uniform
  requires men to wear a baseball cap, are you inadvertently saying that men with dreadlocks don't belong? Are
  you including a prayer space for your employees in your
  new construction plans, if not are you saying that those
  who might want to pray during working hours, are not
  welcome?

- Those who are wedded to equality, rather than equity, will always counter the necessity for equity, with **Whataboutery**, which occurs when someone protests at what they think is inconsistency; and they refuse to act in one instance unless similar action is taken in other similar instances. An example of this is the #BlackLivesMatter movement and the subsequent #AllLivesMatter response or when an attempt to balance the seesaw and create equity is shared and comments arise like 'What about young white working-class boys?' or 'What about those who are disabled?' This type of comment can shut you down, so it's helpful to have a response ready like – 'We live in a society that favours white, heterosexual, **cisgender**, able-bodied, males. Anything that we can do to change that narrative and balance things up is important to do'.

- Fear and discomfort in naming the problem could be one of your blind spots. Many organisations will tolerate the word sexist being using within their walls but are not OK with the word racist being said. If you can't use the words, how can you describe the experience? It is important to articulate a problem so that you can do something about it.

- Your employee resource groups can be a space to notice blind spots in intersectionality. Look at how intersectional identities are showing up in your employee resource groups or not. For example, if your LGBTQ+ employee resource group has a membership of white colleagues only, why might that be happening?

- Those who are leaving are a useful source of information on your blind spots. Ensure that you are identifying the real reason behind colleagues' attrition and that exit interviews are effective. Check whether there are teams where colleagues from the global majority never thrive and how long your colleagues from the global majority stay compared to their white counterparts.

- Looking for themes and clusters of complaints and grievances and examining your complaints and grievance processes may reveal some blind spots. Are complaints coming through and how much trust do colleagues have in the complaints and grievance process?

Many experiences of racism or discrimination go unreported because those who report don't believe that a positive outcome will come from it. In fact, employment tribunals in the UK saw a 48% rise in the number of race discrimination claims in 2020, according to new data stemming from a Freedom of Information request. As a senior diversity, equity, and inclusion specialist said 'you must understand that if those from the global majority become the source of discomfort – it only impedes their progress'. So, there aren't reasons for them not to do so.

The government's most recent survey of Employment Tribunal Applications (2018) found that discrimination cases are some of the least successful types of hearings. Their survey revealed that:

- Only 26% of discrimination cases that went to a full tribunal hearing in 2018 were successful.

- In general, discrimination cases were more likely to be withdrawn/dismissed or settled than to go to a hearing (according to 2017 data).

These statistics illuminate how imperative it is to have support in place for those who do make a complaint, such as:

- Well-being support for those from the global majority.

- An Employee Assistance Programme with counsellors who are experts in **racial trauma**.

- Union representatives educated in diversity, equity and inclusion, and anti-racist practices.

- The ability to report incidences anonymously and helplines.

Many organisations diligently follow up on complaints and grievances, which are quite rightly confidential, but this confidentiality can look like nothing is being done to those not involved. More could be done to share themes or data in a transparent way, helping staff to know that action is being taken and as a result build trust and faith in the system, as well as sending a message of being an organisation that does what it says it will.

Limited opportunities can lead to pigeonholing especially when opportunities and promotions given to people from the global majority are always related to diversity, equity, and inclusion, rather than their specific expertise. This is a blinkered approach to unlocking their talent, look beyond ethnicity to their skills, competence, and capability. Ensure that you don't just recruit staff from the global majority in certain roles such as equity, diversity, and inclusion roles or accountancy.

As you can see there are many areas where you may have blind spots, so getting feedback from suppliers, customers, and stakeholders can help as they can be hard to spot yourself.

3. LEARNING FROM YOUR COLLEAGUES

In the mind of the expert there are few possibilities, in the mind of the beginner there are many. (Suzuki)

A huge part of this journey is stepping away from being the expert, many leaders are promoted because of their technical expertise or specialist expertise, and then need to develop different skills as leaders. To lead, doesn't mean to know it all, but it does mean you need to have a willingness to learn and be vulnerable. You need to search for the good stuff, it will be taking place in your organisation, it's up to you to find it and amplify it.

Add this to the list of qualities mentioned in Chapter Three, 'Being an Empathetic Changemaker', in particular radical humbling and seeking alternative truths. It all comes down to you owning and embodying your choice to be the best leader that you can be.

Examples of How You Can Learn from Your Colleagues

Listen to dissenters – you will have lots to learn from those who don't agree with you. The challenge is not to listen for what you want to hear, but to remember that alternative truths can exist simultaneously.

Part of the process of actively listening is to notice the silences and silent people, those silent resistors – the people who feel hard done – by the emphasis on balancing the seesaw. Engage with them as allies, champions and mentors, sponsors, and experts. Don't ignore their thoughts and feelings but help them to recognise that their experience of being able to avoid conversations about race and ethnicity is the definition of privilege.

Dismissing comments from colleagues can demotivate, demoralise, and invalidate their feelings. Instead, you can thank and appreciate and say things like 'thank you for your challenge' or 'thanks for that different perspective' and still share yours.

Listen to colleagues' lived experience – one organisation that we worked with ran an online session for staff from the global majority to share their experience of discrimination and bias in the workplace. They shared in conversation with each other; white managers and other colleagues observed the conversation but were not permitted to speak or comment. The result was an emotive and visceral experience for those who had never heard these stories before, there was some shock that it could happen in their organisation and they hadn't noticed. This worked in a positive way to engage the silent resistors to recognise the injustice in their place of work and do something about it. Not everyone was swayed, but this powerful listening exercise made a difference. There was considerable emotional labour, bravery, and vulnerability needed by the colleagues from the global majority who shared their experience, and this type of intervention needs to be carefully managed and supported, and as I mentioned previously, relying on colleagues to share their lived experience over and over is not healthy for them. In fact, there is evidence that **racial trauma** can leave people from the global majority with post-traumatic stress disorder.[1]

Consider what the obstacles to you learning from your colleagues from the global majority might be. What might be getting in the way of you listening and learning? One barrier could be **accent bias,** research[2] by Queen Mary University found that Birmingham accents and those from the Caribbean were deemed less intelligent sounding than other accents, this can get in the way of being heard and being taken seriously. Recognise that your bias may mean that you privilege certain accents above others when listening.

Tap into diverse wisdom, the wisdom from cultures, religions and people that you wouldn't have naturally turned to before.

Recognise that there will be some people who are more knowledgeable than you, seek them out and tap into their wisdom. There will also be communities, such as religious groups, that you don't have access to that your colleagues from the global majority might be able to tap into. Many organisations have had to issue apologies due to **cultural appropriation** or offensive messaging; for example is Gucci in 2018 faced backlash over its products, when it released a wool balaclava jumper, that featured a mouth cut out and red panels that looked like exaggerated lips, which resembled **blackface**. If only they had a diverse mix of people in the room, and an equitable environment where all voices were valued and heard, they could have avoided this.

EXPERIMENT TO FIND WHAT WORKS

Advancing racial equity requires wise solutions. Those solutions will rise out of the novel connections created in human minds. Those human minds can only make novel connections if new stuff is entering those minds. New stuff only enters our minds if you're curious. And to be curious is to be willing to experiment and fail in service of succeeding.

Curiosity is critical for great leadership. Curious leaders create a culture of curiosity. People are encouraged to probe, ask, investigate, invent, explore, experiment, be enthusiastically inquisitive, and fail, in order to foster creativity and innovation.

Examples of Experimenting to Find What Works

Firstly, ensure that you have **psychological safety** in which to operate. Psychological safety is the held belief that you will not suffer any negative consequences through taking interpersonal risks. This may include speaking up with an idea in a meeting, challenging the status quo, making a change, or admitting a mistake. Once this is in place:

Don't be afraid to try new things and to take risks – we all know that it can feel uncomfortable, pushing yourself outside your comfort zone to try or learn new things, especially as a leader in an organisation. Organisations like the Chartered Institute of Personnel and Development (CIPD) provide guides on how to talk about race at work. I would recommend sharing your intention for the conversation, and being open about how you feel. For example, 'My intention is to support you, I don't want to say the wrong thing, I am happy for you to correct me if I do'.

Be adventurous – read a challenging book together – such as *White Fragility* or *Why I am no longer talking to white people about race*. Walk through a neighbourhood that you don't usually go to and take in the cultural differences, such as shops that might stock different food and products to where you live, or volunteer to support groups from a different community to your own. Even rotating the chairperson of your next meeting can be a good start.

- Ask questions – rather than simply accepting the status quo, don't be afraid to ask questions and to dig a little deeper. Children are fantastic at doing this, 'why is the grass green?', 'why is the sky blue?', 'why do I have to go to school?' they ask all the good questions that you stop asking in adulthood. Here are some potential questions, however, don't be limited by them, go where your curiosity takes you:

- What makes you say that colleague doesn't have management potential?

- What makes you say that they are not a good fit?

- What makes you think it will take longer to get them up to speed than another colleague?

- Does your name have special meaning?

- I'd like to find out more about the month of Ramadan where do you suggest that I start?

Seek newness – recognise the moments that you feel uncomfortable, that's often when you are experiencing something new. These are opportunities to experiment. When you go to your next networking event, seek out the person you are least inclined to talk to instead of sticking to the comfortable clique that you usually spend time with, and see what comes from it. One manager that I have worked with, fasts for one day of Ramadan and breaks fast with their colleague and family, this helps them understand the experience of fasting while still having to carry on with everyday work and life. They have developed increased empathy, as well as understanding that fasting is just one small element of what Ramadan is about.

Your efforts at being curious may not always go as you plan, but there will always be learning, so love, love, love those teachable moments and create a culture that searches for those moments of growth.

Find ways to celebrate when you see good practice; a letter from the CEO, internal awards, enhanced job titles like ambassador or champion can all help staff feel valued for doing the right thing. Don't get me wrong, no one should engage in this work for the accolades, but celebrating sends a wider message of the behaviour that you value in your organisation.

As you expand your knowledge of your colleagues lived experience, reveal your blind spots and what you know about racial equity in your organisation. These form the sandbags to create equilibrium on the seesaw for the push and pull of equity and once you know where you are, you can start re-balancing the seesaw.

APPRECIATING DIFFERENCE

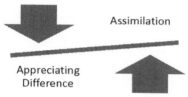

Increasing your appreciation of difference and decreasing your need for colleagues from the global majority to assimilate will help you move from expecting everyone to be a certain type and fit in to appreciating, noticing, and valuing difference which will help balance the seesaw.

Some ways in which you can balance the seesaw are:

Decolonise your thinking and action by balancing the valuing of knowledge and experience between the global south and the global north. So that it doesn't appear that the global north is the right way, and the global south is the wrong way. Many educational institutions are working to decolonise their curriculum so that research is not so European centric, and organisations should consider where they obtain their methods, processes, and intelligence from too. Just because the lived experience of your colleagues from the global majority may be different to yours, it doesn't mean that they are not intelligent, in fact if they were in the majority group you would need to adapt to their way of thinking, doing, and being! English is still the language of many businesses, but what if your rhythms and accent were not seen as the norm, would you like to be ignored, seen as less intelligent, and less able to contribute and have your sentences re-explained incorrectly? Appreciate others belonging alongside your belonging by reading books from diverse British authors David Olusoga, Nikesh Shukla, and Afua Hirsch which explain the impact of those from the global majority on British history, if this is an area that you need to learn more about.

Support your 'onlys', it can be isolating to be the only person from your background in a department, team or organisation, and this isolation can fuel **imposter syndrome**, the feeling that the person is a fraud and will be found out to not be as good as expected. When you are a visible minority, **imposter syndrome** can be more acute. How people behave in your presence, whether you are acknowledged or ignored, whether you are included, whether your ideas are heard or dismissed, whether people can remember your name, and other subtle acts indicate whether you feel like an imposter or not. Another challenge is that you can feel hyper visible and invisible at the same time. Highly visible for your mistakes but overlooked when it comes to promotions and opportunities. As a result, it can be really difficult to relax and be truly yourself in an environment where you don't know if you will be accepted as you are, as there is no one like you.

To support those who are the 'only' one from their background in your team, department, organisation, find out what support they might need, such as a coach, mentor, and counsellor from a similar background and alongside that, work on increasing representation of those from the global majority. Your colleague may want to help you build representation, but don't assume that they do, as this would be in addition to their day job and might not be of interest to them or they may not want to get drawn in to being the 'diversity' person.

Assuming is dangerous – when you are making efforts to advance racial equity you can fall into the trap of thinking that you understand the experience of those from the global majority, perhaps you've decided that the South Asian woman in the meeting is not speaking up because she is timid or deferential to authority so needs to be encouraged to speak, when maybe she just has nothing to add. Everyone's experience is different, the experience of the woman with South Asian heritage who lived in India until she was age 20 and came to the UK to study and the woman who was born in the UK to South Asian parents is different, because the first woman would not have experienced being in a minority until she was 20, but even if they both had exactly the same life experience the way that they see the world will be unique to them. Another common mistake is to assume someone whose heritage is Black African and someone whose heritage is Black Caribbean has the same experience; the cultures are very different.

Don't weaponise – if you have a difficult message to give to a colleague or colleagues from the global majority, do not seek out a colleague from the global majority to deliver this message, it is a form of weaponising race and ethnicity. Especially, if the thinking is that the receiver of the message will be less resistant to the message coming from someone with a similar background.

Seek out and reward difference – open yourself up to different opinions and perspectives and watch the creativity blossom. Scientists have measured the amount of data that enters the brain and found that an average person living today processes as much as 74 GB in information a day (i.e. as much as watching 16 movies), through TV, computers, mobile phones, tablets, billboards, and many other gadgets, as a result we have to make quick decisions about what is important and what isn't.

We all have well-trodden pathways in our brain that have helped us make quick decisions and sort through the plethora of information that we receive each day. To unlearn what has served us for a long time is not easy, but it is possible if you are motivated to do so. After all we once believed smoking to be good for us, used encyclopaedias instead of searching the internet for everything, and didn't think we needed seatbelts in our cars.

These well-trodden pathways serve you, but also get in the way when you want to change your ways of thinking and start noticing things like inequity in your workplace. It takes conscious and intentional effort to disrupt your usual ways of thinking. You must be planful about this and create nudges to develop new habits.

Three things that you can do:

1 Have lunch or coffee catch-ups with different and diverse
   groups of people.

2 **Mentor** or **sponsor** someone who is from the global majority
   and has a different background to your own.

3 Encourage 'wildcard' comments, ask colleagues if they have
   a left field idea, encourage them to play devil's advocate, and
   share what they think might be missing in your thinking. You
   could engage in this playfully, after all we learn best when we
   are at play and relaxed, you could even give a prize or have a
   leader board for the person who comes up with the most wildcard comments per month.
       Welcome these comments by saying something like 'interest-
   ing perspective let's take 5 mins to explore it' or even 'that's
   really challenged how I see the world, can I sleep on it and
   come back to you tomorrow'.

It generally takes courage and positive intent for someone to share
their truth with you, if they do, and they are then punished for it,
they may hold back from doing so again. You could reward the person with acknowledgement and say, 'your contribution has opened
my eyes', or 'I think more people need to hear this perspective'.

You've Been Cancelled, Now What? – Some organisations
have received negative media attention due to poor judgement regarding their suppliers, advertising campaigns, or
performative media statements, and in our current society, these organisations get 'cancelled' and customers vote
with their feet. Smart organisations publicly apologise and
privately do the work to be better, however, the negative
impact on their reputation can stay with them for some
time. A mistake they often make is to then request that their
colleagues from the global majority act as their advocates,

this is too much for colleagues in addition to their day jobs and not fair to do so. Instead, everyone should take on this burden, and if it falls disproportionately on those from the global majority because they are on the front line, then specific colleagues, teams, and departments should be employed with a role to deal with the questions around this. Lastly, working in an environment, which the outside world believes is racist, will carry considerable emotional labour for your colleagues, it's important for you to consider the support that you can provide, such as counselling, or support groups and ensure that the counsellors are from a variety of backgrounds to fully understand your colleagues lived experience. Maybe you think that this couldn't happen to your organisation, unfortunately if you don't have the right voices (global majority voices) in the room, the risk of your blind spots is high.

CHALLENGING THE STATUS QUO

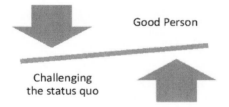

Every organisation needs a truth teller and an educator and they need to be brave. (Dr Alaettin Çarıkcı, Vodafone UK, Diversity and Inclusion Manager)

I assume that you are a good person, doing the best that you can with the resources that you have at your disposal, but being a good person isn't enough, if you are not taking action. Without taking action you are condoning the status quo of racial inequity in your organisation.

Inclusive Recruitment

If we were being truthful in recruitment, it would sound something like this:

"As a person from the global majority in the workplace in this organisation and the team that you will be joining, it's likely that

(1) people will question your skills and abilities;
(2) stereotype and misinterpret your behaviours;
(3) not sponsor and advocate for you in the way they will for your white peers; and
(4) people will either treat you as odd or exotic.

This behaviour will lead you to question yourself, eat away at your confidence, and have people telling you that you have imposter syndrome. Now do you want this exciting opportunity?"

Inclusive recruitment is one of the essential components in which you can challenge the status quo, although a culture of inclusion is what will retain your colleagues. Inclusive recruitment requires that you remove the bias in your recruitment process, a common issue is that degree qualifications from particular institutions, or from other countries may not be valued highly, even though they are equal according to the awarding bodies. As Asif Sadiq, MBE says 'Ultimately recruitment decisions come down to one person' which is then subject to their biases.

Organisational norms are reinforced in recruitment, you may convince yourself that the best candidate got the role, but what about the process, language, and interactions that advantaged a particular candidate. This is a key place to re-balance that seesaw. Including inclusion questions in interviews shows its importance and makes it foremost in the minds of your candidates too, you could ask: Tell me about a time when you advocated for diversity and inclusion in the workplace or can you give me an example of how you make your direct reports feel a sense of inclusion, belonging, and equity on a daily basis?

Ensure that at least 15–20% of the candidates for your roles are from the global majority and ensure you have diverse recruitment panels with equal decision-making power. Section 159 of the Equality Act 2010 allows an employer to treat an applicant or employee with a protected characteristic (e.g. race, sex, or age) more favourably in connection with recruitment or promotion than someone without that characteristic who is as qualified for the role. The employer must reasonably think that the person with the protected characteristic suffers a disadvantage or is underrepresented in that particular activity. Taking the positive action must be a proportionate means of enabling or encouraging people to overcome the disadvantage or to take part in the activity. Employers must not have a policy of treating people who share a characteristic more favourably; they should decide whether or not to take positive action on a case-by-case basis.

Your recruitment process can help if you have an **ethnicity pay gap** in your organisation, you can ban past salary questions from your interviews, so not to reinforce pay gaps that existed in the persons previous organisation and also publish the salary for the role creating transparency.

Careful of the Model Minority Trap

The model minority trap was mentioned by William Peterson in an article for the *New York Times* Magazine. Peterson used it to describe Japanese Americans as 'a minority that has risen above even prejudiced criticism'. Since then, the term has evolved to encompass all Asian Americans, or, exponentially, all Asian ethnic minorities in the western world. The model minority myth pits those from the global majority against one another and creates a hierarchy in which Asian people are often represented at the top. By putting people from the global majority in competition with one another, the myth detracts us from striving together towards racial equity for all.

Something else to understand is that there can be bias within those from the global majority, whether that be because of **colourism, caste sytems,** class or other aspects of identity.

Advocate for Someone

One way to challenge the status quo is to advocate for someone who you wouldn't usually, someone from the global majority. Think about your career, has anyone every tapped you on the

shoulder and encouraged you to apply for a role, put in a good
word for you, helped you showcase your skills in front of an influential audience, or introduced you to the right people? I imagine
the answer is yes. One influential person in my life was a white
man originally from the USA, his name was Gene Horan, he gave
me a wonderful opportunity to train as a coach, develop my skills
while he was my boss, and I know that he advocated for me when
I wasn't in the room. He was a true developer of people. On paper
there was nothing in common between us, our gender, ethnicity,
nationality, and I believe personality types were different, but he
looked beyond his natural affinity and recognised my potential and
gave me a chance. Sadly, Gene was a victim of COVID-19 and
passed away, but I am forever thankful for his sponsorship. What
an amazing legacy he leaves with me, and I am sure for the many
others that he advocated through his sponsorship. You can be what
Gene was for me and address who benefits from sponsorship, allyship, and mentoring in your organisation. According to research,[3]
59% of Black women have never – not once – had an informal
interaction with a senior leader at their company; less than half
(47%) of white women are in the same position. This highlights
one of the reasons why inequity in the workplace persists, while
also highlighting an entry point to change things. Remember that
any support that you put in place is never to fix your colleagues
from the global majority, but to help address systemic inequality
which may have held them back while you work on addressing it
more widely within your organisation.

Develop Racial Fluency

Having the language that you need to challenge the status quo is
crucial, and you can do this by developing your **racial fluency**. In a
ground-breaking 2014 study, Dr Doyin Atewologun coined the term
'race fluency' in response to research findings that organisations
and their leaders are clearer and more confident about articulating
talent management strategies related to gender than about race. If
you asked me to speak some words in Mandarin, I would trip over
my words, as they aren't familiar, talking about race and ethnicity
requires the same level of intention and practice to become fluent.

You can't leave **racial fluency** to chance; organisations must actively seek to improve the ability of all staff to talk about race and ethnicity. Something worth noting is that many people from the global majority may be developing their racial fluency too, they may not be used to discussing race and ethnicity at work and may not have discussed it much in other spaces either. They may be developing their thoughts and feelings about race and ethnicity in conjunction with their white counterparts.

NOTICE THE INTERSECTIONS

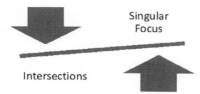

So much of the equity, diversity, and inclusion work has had a singular focus such as gender, disability, or ethnicity, but smart organisations are waking up to the intersections, the diversity within diversity, that reveal where true inequities lie.

Organisations should understand the employee life cycle, including service users, customers and external suppliers now and in the future.

In addition, smart and forward-thinking organisations will be asking what intersectionality looks like in future markets or globally and exploring who their current and future state consumers will be. They will need to think carefully about whether their current actions or inaction around racial equity could exclude their future customers in some way.

Something that isn't talked about much is those who might be **white passing**. For example, someone who has mixed heritage both global majority and white or another example is someone whose features and skin colouring – means that they could be mistaken for being white. These colleagues are in a unique position to use their advantages that come with perceived 'whiteness' to challenge the status quo and speak up for those who can't, while recognising that their experience will be different to someone who is discriminated against because of the colour of their skin.

Looking at the contrasting headlines that Meghan Markle received in comparison to Kate Middleton. They both married into the British Royal Family, however Meghan's Mum is an African American and her Dad is white, whereas both of Kate Middleton's parents are white. It's difficult not to see the negative treatment that Meghan has received as a result. Or the US President admitting the first Black woman to the Supreme Court and the uproar that ensued.

The Black female experience is one intersection that has started to be researched more, the hatred of black females actually has its own term - **Misogynoir**, which highlights the extent of the problem. The Runnymede Trust recently published extensive research on the experience of women from the global majority in the workplace.

The Runnymede Trust found that:

- Institutional racism is common in all sectors and in all organisations: 75% of women from the global majority have experienced racism at work, with 27% having suffered racial slurs.

- Forced to mould to conform: 61% report changing themselves to 'fit-in' at work, from the language or words they use (37%), their hairstyle (26%), and even their name (22%).

- Well-being is being impacted: 39% of women from the global majority stated their well-being had been impacted by a lack of progression compared to 28% of white women, while being refused promotion led to loss of motivation for 43% of women from the global majority.

- Locked out of progression: 28% of women from the global majority (compared with 19% of white women) reported that a manager had blocked their progression at work, and 42% reported being passed over for promotion despite good feedback (compared to 27% for white women).

- Recruitment discrimination: 52% of women from the global majority experience discrimination – such as, being asked for UK qualifications or English as a first language and being asked for ethnicity information outside of monitoring processes.

In 2020, while white women in the USA earn 81 cents for every dollar a white man earns, the same figure for American Indian, Alaska Native, Black, African American, and Hispanic women is 75 cents.[4]

Research from the UK has shown that **LGBTQI+** people's experience of sexual harassment and assault at work varied significantly on their ethnicity. Around a third of white women reported unwanted touching. The percentage of lesbian, bisexual, and trans Black and minority ethnic women who experience unwanted touching is 54%.[5]

People with disabilities, especially those from underrepresented groups, are overrepresented in the ranks of the unemployed. Data from the 2018 Annual Disability Statistics Compendium showed that 73.7% of US African Americans without disabilities had a job, the percentage of US African Americans with disabilities who had a job was 28.6%.[6]

I hope that seeing this stark data implores you to take action and recognise this as a business imperative.

DEVELOPMENTAL INTERVENTIONS

Any strategy to advance racial equity and create a just and fair workplace for all, must connect with the head, the heart, and the hands. It requires a learning culture.

For the head, it must have a firm foundation of data and logic as to why this course of action is the right one – the what and the why.

For the heart, it should connect with the audience on an emotional and visceral sense, motivating them to want to change.

And for the hands, it should provide skills, tools, and behavioural effort, so that action takes place.

In my experience, leaders and managers often find the concept of equity challenging, as they want to treat all of their colleagues the same because in their mind that is just and fair, and they don't want to be accused of favouritism. The truth is that even with that positive intention, you are unlikely to be treating everyone the same, and even if you were it wouldn't achieve the equity of outcomes that we are seeking.

Below I share a range of interventions from zero cost and self-directed to those that require a larger financial investment, as well as resources and interventions tailored to your needs. The important thing for you is to ensure that you reach all levels of your organisation. If you just focus on your pipeline of global majority colleagues, you send the message that it's them who need fixing, if you just focus on the senior leadership team then you risk the chance of the learning not cascading through to the day-to-day operations. Middle managers are a key audience to develop as they can influence the careers of so many colleagues, they can be the concrete ceiling or the hand up. They are often given minimal support to advance equity, and this can compete with their day-to-day deadlines that they prioritise, the key is to integrate advancing racial equity into everything that you do and then it never feels like an addition.

Whatever route you take, measuring impact is essential, you need to know how far you've travelled and what made the most significant positive impact.

STRATEGIC INTERVENTIONS

When change comes from the top of the organisation with a clear strategy, it shows commitment and provides everyone with the clarity to take action. The strategy should be embodied, operationalised, and closely monitored, creating a framework for behaviours at work, in parallel with working to change hearts and minds.

The Parker Review[7] of the ethnic diversity of FTSE boards took place in 2015/2016 and set out its target in 2017 to appoint at least one director from a the global majority on each FTSE 100 Board by 2021 and on each FTSE 250 Board by 2024.

In 2022, looking across the FTSE 100, 164 of the 1,056 director positions (i.e. 16% of them) are held by people from the global majority. This demonstrates progress, particularly over the last two years. However, the great majority of global majority directors are in non-executive director roles. At a Board level, the social element of environmental, social, and corporate governance creates an opportunity to discuss racial equity at senior board level in organisations and The RACE Code[8] – which stands for reporting, action, composition, and education – creates a framework in which Boards can assess where they are in relation to the code and create an action plan to ensure that they are at the minimum, compliant.

The creation of a racial equity plan can put a theory of change into action to achieve a collective vision of what racial equity looks like in your organisation. Plans can drive institutional and structural change, as long as action is taken.

Mapping your employee lifecycle will provide a summary of the collection of encounters your employees have with their colleagues, managers, and HR, from the first day they apply to an open position to the day they leave your organisation.

It includes recruitment, onboarding, performance, development, retention, and off-boarding, and can help you to identify the areas of improvement.

Diversifying your supply chain can also demonstrate your wider commitment to racial equity, beyond just the internal. The large UK Supermarket chain Sainsbury's recently announced that it will invest £1 million in the UK's retail first incubator programme for Black-led businesses, demonstrating that it is not just working to change things internally but at all stages of the supply chain.

Showing commitment to the community outside and inside your organisation sends a strong message of commitment to change. In many parts of the UK, there are areas of affluence and areas of deprivation side by side. Investing in your local community through outreach, support for start-up businesses, school leavers and graduates shows the congruence between internal and external work that the organisation is doing.

Key performance indicators (KPIs) can help keep the focus on addressing racial inequity, but it is not just what is done but the way that it is done, so if the KPIs serve to punish or make people engage at a surface level, that might not be the right approach.

SELF-DIRECTED

There is so much that you and your colleagues can do to develop your understanding of racial equity.

Some organisations allocate learning time each week to staff, so that they can be led by their curiosity and interest to watch TEDx talks, listen to podcasts, and watch relevant movies or documentaries.

You could start a book club and read books together like *Me and White Supremacy* by Layla F. Saad (2020) and work through it. This approach enables your colleagues to work on the areas that are most challenging for them rather than have a one-size-fits-all approach. In order to cascade the learning through the team and organisation, creating a space to discuss key insights from the self-directed learning should also be factored in. Or you could provide staff with credits to use on relevant development of their choice, perhaps a pick and mix or modular approach.

USE LIFE EXPERIENCES

Hearing about the lived experience of your colleagues from the global majority directly from them is a very engaging and immediate way to develop your understanding of their experience.

However, consider how much of this you need to hear, are you addicted to hearing more and more, when is it enough, and how might it be negatively impacting the person sharing their experience? Your reaction also matters, any dismissing, minimising, or defensiveness on your part will mean that the person sharing will not be open to doing so in the future.

That said there are some very successful ways of doing this in the workplace:

Reciprocal mentoring – this is a development intervention that stems from the models of traditional mentoring but is not the same. The pairs are equal partners in the process of learning and the relationship is reciprocal. The approach aims to focus on systemic change as well as at an individual level focussed on race and ethnicity, the person from the global majority will share their experience, gain exposure to a typically more senior colleague while also helping their colleague to better understand the organisational challenges around inequity.

Virtual reality (VR) experiences allow you to walk in someone else's shoes. For this reason, VR is being used by some businesses as part of unconscious bias training. VR can give you the opportunity to experience how certain biases play out in different situations. You can get to understand how biases look and feel, and develop your own methods for tackling these.

Real life immersion - there is no substitute for experience and taking colleagues out of their comfort zone can create a memorable behaviour-changing experience. Visiting exhibitions, galleries, communities and religious buildings can provide that unbeatable real-life immersion.

Listening Circles/Focus Groups – Listening circles offer a safe space for individuals to open up and share their thoughts, emotions, experiences, and challenges without fear of being judged. By practising open listening and offering full acceptance in this way, you can build a sense of psychological safety and trust in the workplace which in turn, naturally boosts a sense of community and belonging.

Focus groups can reveal what you know deep down but have never spoken about. If you don't have colleagues from the global majority, or they are not willing to participate, you can find pre-recorded materials of those from the global majority sharing their experience in your sector or this is something that you could engage an external company to provide for you.

TRAINING AND DEVELOPMENT

Most organisations don't have the internal capacity, knowledge, expertise, and diverse facilitation team to deliver the training necessary to advance racial equity in their organisation. There is definitely a wealth of resources out there that you can use or you can engage an external provider. If you do engage an external provider for this work do ensure that they have a track record in this space and can provide information on impact and references. A founder who is part of the global majority is ideal, with a team that is representative of the intersectional ethnic diversity that you are trying to impact in your organisation. The external provider should be willing to work in partnership with you to bespoke development to your needs. By choosing the right external provider you can enhance the credibility of the programme of training and development, as internal staff often value an external perspective and by allocating budget you prove your commitment.

Fundamental Programmes

Fundamental programmes give the basics on which to work from, they might not create sustainable behavioural change, but they will increase awareness and ensure that everyone is equipped with the basic knowledge they need.

Fundamental programmes include courses on unconscious bias which aim to raise awareness of the mental shortcuts that lead to snap judgements of a person's talent or character, these judgements are often based on race, ethnicity and gender. The goal of this type of training is to reduce bias in attitudes and behaviours at work, from hiring and promotion decisions to interactions with customers and colleagues.

Cultural intelligence and inclusion training transfers the foundational knowledge, skills, and mindsets required to work effectively with culturally diverse stakeholders and to foster culturally inclusive work settings. Whether you want to explore global cultural differences or more local cultural difference due to ethnicity, this can be a good place to start.

Anti-racism training provides education about systemic racism and empowers you to identify the sources and tactics of resistance to dismantle racism and to discuss the stages and characteristics of anti-racist organisational development. It provides a framework for understanding racism. It will include training on bias and privilege and can include how to talk about race and ethnicity.

Behavioural Change Programmes

Once you have the fundamentals in place, behavioural change programmes are the way to go, or you might use these interventions with individuals and smaller groups in conjunction with the fundamental development for the wider organisation.

Coaching – whether one-to-one or team coaching, coaching is all about facilitating change and is a powerful way of creating those realisations and lightbulb moments that create lasting change.

According to the Association for Coaching, 'coaching is a collaborative solution-focussed, results-orientated and systematic process in which the coach facilitates the enhancement of work performance, life experience, self-directed learning and personal growth of the coachee'. It's a particularly useful intervention for time poor senior leaders who want to do the work that makes them feel vulnerable around equity and inclusion in private before they go public. Coaching can be a very helpful intervention for those who take on the voluntary role of leading or Chairing an employee resource group, these people are often thrust into meetings with senior people. One-to-one coaching can help them have the confidence, skills and strategies to navigate those conversations. Team coaching is impactful for groups of managers to unpack their challenges around racial equity, helping them with support and solutions. Not any coach will do, coaches must be inclusive, demonstrate racial fluency, understand cultural variance in verbal and non-verbal expression, and create trust by acknowledging their and their clients' ethnicity and culture. In short, you must create equity in your coaching pool too.

Allyship Programmes – the right policies alone cannot shift workplace culture. It's critical that the whole workforce becomes part of the cause, that's where allyship comes in. Research shows allies don't just influence one person at a time. They inspire others to act as change agents, too, creating a culture of acceptance and support.[9] Simply put, allyship is a powerful force for good.

Advancing your pipeline of future talent from the global majority – some organisations are making use of Section 158 of the Equality Act to deliver development programmes specifically for their talent from the global majority. Section 158 of the Equality Act 2010 allows employers to take action to compensate for disadvantages that it reasonably believes are faced by people who share a particular protected characteristic (i.e. age, disability, gender reassignment, marriage and civil partnership, pregnancy and maternity, race, religion or belief, and sex or sexual orientation). Separate provisions allowing positive action in relation to recruitment and promotion in limited circumstances are contained in Section 159 of the Act.

Case Study: The Power of Positive Action Programmes

In 2021, talent from the global majority at Coventry City Council represented just 19% of its headcount and considerably less at senior leadership level.

It commissioned a positive action programme for top talent from the global majority.

Fifteen talented staff from the global majority were recruited on to the programme, following a rigorous application process. They then embarked on a programme of taught sessions, action learning, sponsorship and line manager involvement. Evaluations after the programme ended found that...

- 100% now feel that they can be themselves at work (compared to 21% at the start of the programme).

- 100% can now talk to their line manager about race and ethnicity (compared to 57% at the start of the programme.

- 100% would recommend the programme to a colleague.

- 30% were promoted during the programme duration and others achieved promotion after the programme completed.

It wasn't just the participants who benefitted from the programme, but the line managers and sponsors did too. A sponsor said ...

'It has enabled me to see things from a different perspective. I've learnt about how important culture and diversity is. I hadn't thought previously about the impact that coming from a different cultural background might have on your working life'.

It is important to integrate any positive action programmes that you deliver into your talent framework, and ensure that they sit central to your talent strategy.

Sponsorship programmes are designed to match talent from the global majority with senior leaders, who have the power, position, and political intelligence to advocate for their progression. Formalising what the many white colleagues receive informally to balance that seesaw.

Some thoughts on development interventions:

- Don't passively consume training and development, encourage all to actually engage with it.

- Don't expect instant change, your colleagues from the global majority may not be used to having equal weight on the seesaw, so it will take some getting used to. Commit to three years of development and then measure the impact.

- Ensure the interventions touch all employee groups at all levels.

NOTES

1. Carter, R. T. (2007, January 1). Racism and Psychological and Emotional Injury: Recognizing and Assessing Race-Based Traumatic Stress. Otolaryngology-Head and Neck Surgery, 35(1), 646–649. https://doi.org/10.1016/j.otohns.2005.10.050.

2. https://www.qmul.ac.uk/media/news/2019/hss/accent-bias-exists-but-people-can-resist-the-urge-to-discriminate.html

3. LeanIn.Org and McKinsey & Company. (2018). *Women in the workplace*. Unpublished data.

4. Payscale. (2022, March 15). "2022 State of the Gender Pay Gap Report." Retrieved from https://www.payscale.com/research-and-insights/gender-pay-gap/

5. A TUC Report. (2019). Chapter 1. Sexual Harassment in the Workplace: An Overview. In Unwelcome and unlawful (pp. 8–18). doi: 10.7591/9781501732454-002

6. Institute on Disability / UCED. "2018 Annual Disability Statistics Compendium." 2018 Annual Disability Statistics Compendium | Annual Disability Statistics Compendium. Retrieved from https://disabilitycompendium.org/compendium/2018-annual-disability-statistics-compendium. Accessed on October 23, 2022.

7. Parker, J. (2022, March 16). *Improving the ethnic diversity of UK boards. An update on the Parker review*. The Parker Review Committee.

8. The RACE Code – which stands for **Reporting, Action, Composition and Education** – was established in 2020 by Dr Karl George MBE to help organisations improve race equality and to tackle discrimination within the workplace.

9. Heilman, M. E., & Hayes, M. C. (2005). No credit where credit is due: Attributional rationalization of women's success in male-female teams. *Journal of Applied Psychology, 90*(5), 905–926; Heilman, M. E. (2012). Gender stereotypes and workplace bias. *Research in Organizational Behavior, 32*, 113–135.

Chapter Five

PRACTISING THOUGHTFUL INTROSPECTION

We have travelled through the stages of advancing racial equity in the workplace expanding our Awareness of the context, Deepening our knowledge of others, being an Empathetic changemaker, defining our Pathways to action, and now to practising Thoughtful introspection.

Although I have provided examples, suggestions, and practical steps throughout this book, there is no doubt that this work starts with you at a very personal level, to do the deep work necessary to be brave and bold in this complex and messy world.

It can be disruptive to your self-image to consider how systemic racism has impacted your long held thoughts and actions and also that you will have done some things that have hurt others, made them suffer unnecessarily in the workplace and beyond, potentially stagnated their career, and othered them. We can often feel shame and guilt about our past behaviour, but we cannot go back in time and change what has been done.

CALLING IN

I recall an example when studying on a course, a fellow mature student wasn't happy with the grade that they had been given, and so decided to write a scathing attack with some racial undertones on a lecturer and the course via the online portal that we used. I and the other students read in horror and none of us stepped in to the lecturer's defence, we were **passive bystanders**. We rationalised our behaviour with thoughts like the lecturer could defend themselves, someone else would step in, it wasn't our place. When I reflect back I know that it was definitely our place to say something and be an **active bystander** when someone is being attacked in this way. By saying nothing we were condoning the behaviour of the disgruntled student. I do feel guilty about that.

American Researcher, Brené Brown, makes a distinction between shame and guilt. She describes shame as feelings of being unworthy and flawed, when we feel like this we remove ourselves or the people that make us feel that way. In the workplace, that can look like the person from the global majority, who was already being side-lined, now being moved to another team because of their manager's feeling of shame about the way that they've treated them. The manager can also become defensive because they don't want to admit that they have made a mistake, and so decide that everything that is said or done by the person from the global majority is a personal attack.

Instead of shame and the resulting negative coping mechanisms to deal with it, Brecé Brown encourages guilt, which is healthier and more active in orientation. When you have guilt, you know that you did something wrong and acknowledge it and you also know that you will aim to be better in the future and most importantly you mean it. You still recognise that you are flawed and fallible but know that bit by bit you can improve.

If I knew then what I know now, I would have spoken up, or as I like to label it 'called in' rather than 'called out' the angry student, with the aim of educating them and encouraging them to be better than they were before. Shape-shifting racism can be like a disease working through your organisation, vigilance is key and when you see it you must speak out. Here are some ways that I could have done better, that you could adapt to do the same.

You mentioned that you think that your grade was unfair, can you share your thinking around that? What made you call this lecturer out (the only one from the global majority) when you could have spoken to all of the lecturers?

Or

For example, you may not have realised it, in your complaint about your grade, when you commented on how articulate the lecturer was verbally in lectures, it could offend. Why wouldn't a lecturer be articulate, for me there was an implication that because they were from the global majority it was a surprise. If you really want to give them a compliment, you could make it more constructive and something that they could use to enhance the way they do things.

Or

I noticed that you keep calling the lecturer by the wrong name even in writing, I used to find their name difficult, because it was unfamiliar, I know that I wouldn't like it if someone constantly did that to me, I found it challenging at first, but this is how I taught myself to remember it.

Be prepared for the discomfort that you will experience from 'calling in' behaviour, the reward from doing so is that it will become something that comes naturally to you with practice, and also it has the potential to give others the opportunity to change.

CONVERSATIONS ON RACE AND ETHNICITY

It all starts with you, if you are planning to have any conversation about race and ethnicity with your colleagues, it's worth asking yourself the questions that you want others to work on first. Try these for starters:

- How has your racial identity affected your experience as an employee in your organisation positively or negatively?

- How have you felt about the increased focus and conversation about race and ethnicity in society and in the workplace?

- How do you feel that your organisation has responded to the increased awareness of the issue of racial discrimination?

Do answer these questions for yourself, it will help you understand the mental processing required to respond to this type of question. Go beyond your surface level responses to these questions, you may have to keep going back to them over a few days.

Before you speak with colleagues ensure that you have **psychological safety**. Then share your intention for the conversation (why you want to talk about race and ethnicity and what you'd like to take from the conversation), share some of your thinking and reflections from the questions that you have asked yourself in advance of the conversation, being vulnerable will give permission to your colleague to do the same. Trust will only be built if and once you've had the conversation and that you maintain confidentiality, if that's what was agreed between you, and do what you say you will if actions were made. You may have to re-visit conversations as you build trust and depending on your colleague's personality they may want to go away and think about questions that you ask and come back to you.

YOUR REFLECTIVE PRACTICE

This work can be done alone, by buddying with a colleague, or alongside an experienced coach. Daily journaling on these questions on this journey or planning a weekly reflection point can help you keep track of what is going well and what could be even better. Journaling will enhance your reflection. Writing improves your ability to think and is also a great way to track how far you have come on your journey to equity. All you need is a pen, a notebook and an investment of time. You can start with just 5 mins a day, or block of 30 mins a week, and see how it goes for you.

Start With Your Why – Be Purposeful

Friedrich Nietzsche observing those in concentration camps said that 'He who has a why to live can bear almost any how'. Your 'why' serves as a constant motivator to keep you on track. Your 'why' will also inspire others to join you, change hearts and minds, and give the staying power to achieve results and knowing your why for your commitment to racial equity is imperative, if you want to persevere through challenge, resistance, and complexity.

Journal Prompts

- I am motivated to advance racial equity and justice in my workplace because ...

- My real interest in racial equity is ...

- Equity and justice at work is important to me personally because ...

- Racial equity aligns with my values of ...

- The situations that have brought home to me the importance of racial equity and justice at work are ...

- The relationships that I can build to advance racial equity are ...

- The legacy that I would like to leave at work is ...

- The shadow that I would like to cast on others as a leader is ...

We can only persevere when our 'why' is strong enough. Knowing what motivates you helps you align your work with what's important to you. Think about your values, your inner compass, what is most important to you in your work, and how your current role fulfils this.

Identify Your Fears, So That You Won't Be in the Grip of Them

It is unwise to be too sure of one's own wisdom. It is healthy to be reminded that the strongest might weaken and the wisest might err. (Mahatma Gandhi)

If you find that something is holding you back from taking action, it can be worth identifying what that is. It will often be a deep-seated fear or belief that you can't achieve your goal. These prompts will help you identify and minimise those fears.

Journal Prompts

- The thing that I am fearful of and gets in the way of me advancing racial equity is …

- The thing that I would do to advance racial equity at work if I wasn't scared would be …

- I am avoiding certain people, places, situations, conversations, or experiences because I am fearful of …

- When it comes to racial equity, I am uncomfortable talking about … because …

- When advancing racial equity and justice at work, I am afraid people will think of me as …

- I am afraid of being vulnerable in the workplace because …

Some ways to overcome those fears are as follows:

(1) Blow it up: Imagine your fear and blow it out of all proportion. Laughing at fears will help gain control of them. How likely is it that could happen?

(2) Ask Is it true?: What's the evidence for your fear, find ways that disprove it. For example, if your fear is that you will offend someone, ask yourself: How often have I offended people, am I often told that I am emotionally unintelligent?

(3) Expose yourself: Do what scares you, in order to test the validity of your fear. By doing the thing that scares you, you learn that even if it doesn't go to plan, you will survive and most likely also learn something.

(4) Take risks: The purpose is to challenge beliefs that certain behaviours are too dangerous to risk, when reason says that while the outcome is not guaranteed they are worth the chance. For example, if you have trouble with perfectionism or fear of failure, you might start tasks where there is a reasonable chance of failing.

(5) Do the opposite: Behave in the opposite of how you'd usually react. Don't wait until you 'feel like' doing it: practising the new behaviour, will gradually internalise the new habit.

Personal Vision

Your personal vision will give you a mental picture of what success looks like for you and what you want to achieve over time. It provides you with guidance and inspiration as to what to focus on achieving, and it will keep you anchored on what's important.

If you are like me whenever you set off on a car journey to a location that you haven't visited before, you programme the address in to your sat nav for guidance. You don't just randomly start driving and hope to get there, so it would be wise to do the same on your journey to advance racial equity. The most innovative leaders[1] always have a vision.

Journal Prompts

- My journey towards racial equity so far has been …

- What has changed in me, at work, in the world that makes racial equity at work so important to me is …

- I plan to advance racial equity at work by …

- Ideally, racial equity in my workplace will look like …
  (describe it through your five senses: sight, sound, touch, taste, and smell).

- This vision of racial equity at work will make things better for us all by …

- Obstacles that I may experience in my journey to advance racial equity are as follows:

- I will overcome those obstacles through …

- I know that together we can achieve this because …

Once you have your vision, write it down, and read it regularly. You may also want to share it more widely to inspire others to come along on the journey with you.

HUMAN RESOURCES PROFESSIONALS

Human resources have an exciting role to play in advancing racial equity at work:

> *The HR/People function is a key bedrock of any organisation and its and other senior leaders should be curious about why Black, Asian and minority ethnic groups are persistently failing to fill senior and board level positions, compared to their white colleagues. There is a leadership deficit if they aren't curious, especially when the data is available and requires them to act on it. (Peter Alleyne, Associate Director for Diversity, Equity, Inclusion and Race Equality at Rethink Mental Illness)*

Human resources professionals play a significant role in balancing the seesaw as managers are reliant on you, so if you aren't leading then managers can't follow.

We know that human resources can be the first people to blame when something goes wrong, but you can play a role in providing challenge and push back and asking the wider organisation about the role that they are playing in changing things.

We are a powerful point in history where it feels like business has the power to change society and is perhaps more trusted than those elected to the country.

As a human resources professional, you can role model what you want to see and drive change. Share your passion and your vision of the impact change will make. The reverberations of someone from the global majority achieving a role in the C-Suite will impact their generations to come, their community, family, and even the world.

You must ask tough questions of yourself and others:

- How representational is your current and anticipated future workforce?

- What actions do you take at graduate level that creates high representation from the global majority, that you don't do at the middle/senior levels?

- What are you not doing right if only certain people succeed in your organisation?

Final thoughts ...

For real change to happen it is important to put the focus on systemic change and know that it's a journey to get there. I hope that this book has shown that there are multiple perspectives and ways to tackle change. You don't need to choose one way, but try many.

Data alone cannot change the world, tell compelling stories that speak to people's values and identities in order to shift the debate.

Develop your network of influence to individually and collectively make change happen.

Prepare for and then harness external events. The killing of George Floyd was a seminal moment, sadly there will be others, be prepared to harness the energy and goodwill that sparks action from these events in a genuine and sustainable way.

Mobilise everyone to support change, this is not a human resources or diversity, equity, and inclusion professional's problem. If we don't want to stall and ultimately go backwards, equity has to be in everyone's job title. Striving for equality, diversity, and inclusion was the first step but now we must elevate our understanding to achieving equity.

All that your colleagues from the global majority want is:

- To be believed in and to live up to high expectations.

- To be afforded the same opportunity and mistakes as their white colleagues.

- To be valued for their difference.

- To enjoy the push and pull of the seesaw for the good of everyone.

The opposite of love is not hate, it's indifference.

The opposite of art is not ugliness, it's indifference.

The opposite of faith is not heresy, it's indifference.

And the opposite of life is not death, it's indifference. (Elie Wiesel, 1928–2016)

I urge you not to be indifferent, be the one opening the gate, handing out the sandbags, and sharing the power for the benefit of all.

Note

1. Zenger, J., & Folkman, J. (2014, December 15). *Research: 10 Traits of Innovative Leaders. Harvard Business Review.*

GLOSSARY OF TERMS

Accent bias   Unjustifiable discrimination of individuals who speak a language with an accent.

Active Bystander   Someone who chooses to challenge unacceptable or threatening behaviour.

Adultification bias   A form of racial prejudice where children belonging to the global majority, typically Black children, are treated by adults as being more mature than they actually are.

Affinity bias   The tendency people have to connect with others who share similar interests, experiences, and backgrounds.

Ally   Someone who advocates for groups or individuals who are not afforded the same power and privilege as themselves.

Bias   A tendency, inclination, or prejudice towards or against something or someone.

Blackface   Commonly refers to when someone (typically with white skin) paints their face darker to resemble a Black person. It's seen as racist and deeply offensive.

Passive Bystander   A passive bystander is someone who witnesses a racist or biased behaviour but does nothing about it.

Caste system   A class structure that is determined by birth.

Cisgender   A person whose sense of personal identity and gender corresponds with their birth sex.

Colonising   The action or process of settling among and establishing control over the indigenous people of an area.

Colourblindness (racial)   A racial ideology that suggests the best way to end discrimination is by treating individuals as equally as possible, without regard to race, culture, or ethnicity.

Colourism A form of discrimination based on skin tone, which discriminates against dark-skinned people in favour of those with lighter skin from the same race.

Covering Downplaying certain aspects of your identity to fit in and not be stereotyped – Deloitte Uncovering Talent 2018

Critical race theory The idea that race is a social construct, and that racism is not merely the product of individual bias or prejudice, but also something embedded in legal systems and policies. Originated in the mid-1970s in the writings of several American legal scholars.

Cultural appropriation The unacknowledged or inappropriate adoption of the customs, practices, ideas, etc. of one people or society by members of another and typically more dominant people or society.

Decolonisation The process of undoing colonising practices. Within the work context, this means confronting and challenging the colonising practices that have influenced work in the past, and which are still present today.

Diversity In the workplace, refers to an organisation that intentionally employs a workforce comprised of individuals with a range of characteristics, such as gender, religion, race, age, ethnicity, sexual orientation, education, and other attributes.

Employee resource group A voluntary, employee-led diversity and inclusion initiative that is formally supported by an organisation.

Equality The idea that everyone should be treated equally and receive the dignity and respect that they deserve and that their differences are celebrated.

Equity Understanding and giving those from the global majority what they need to achieve equal outcomes. This is achieved by considering systems that disadvantage and seeking to overcome them. To do so we need to take an individual approach, to lead, share power and focus on outcomes. This will balance the seesaw.

Ethnicity Refers to large groups of people classed according to common racial, national, tribal, religious, linguistic, cultural origin or backgrounds, a social construct used to categorise and characterise seemingly distinct populations.

Ethnicity pay gap The difference in the average pay between colleagues from the global majority backgrounds in a workforce, compared to white colleagues.

Gaslighting A form of emotional abuse, it can be used to make the victim question their view of reality and things happening to them which then impacts their mental wellbeing.

Global majority A collective term. It refers to people who are Black, Asian, Brown, dual-heritage, indigenous to the global south, and or have been racialised as 'ethnic minorities'.

Global north Encompasses the rich and powerful regions such as North America, Europe, and Australia.

Global south Refers broadly to the regions of Latin America, Asia, Africa, and Oceania.

Implicit Association Test The assessment of implicit stereotypes held, such as associations between particular racial categories and stereotypes about those groups.

Imposter syndrome A collection of feelings of inadequacy that persist despite evident success, identified by Pauline Clance and Suzanne Rose Imes, 1985.

Inclusion When people feel valued and accepted in their team and in the wider organisation, without having to conform.

Interest convergence A theory coined by the late Derrick Bell, law professor, and spiritual godfather to the field of study known as critical race theory. Interest convergence stipulates that Black people achieve civil rights victories only when white and Black interests converge.

Intergenerational racial pain or trauma A term used to describe a 'passing down' of the traumatic impact and emotional fallout from racism.

Intersectionality Coined in 1989 by professor Kimberlé Crenshaw to describe how race, class, gender, and other individual characteristics 'intersect' with one another and overlap, and the compound effect of that intersection.

LGBTQI+ Refers to lesbian, gay, bisexual, transgender, queer (or sometimes questioning), intersex, and others. The 'plus' represents other sexual identities including pansexual and Two-Spirit.

Mentor A person who provides guidance, advice, and support from their experience.

Meritocracy A system, organisation, or society in which people are chosen and moved into positions of success, power, and influence on the basis of their demonstrated abilities and merit.

Microaggressions Statements, actions, or incidents regarded as an instance of indirect, subtle, or unintentional discrimination against the global majority.

Misogynoir Hatred directed towards Black women where race and gender both play roles in bias. The term was coined by black feminist Moya Bailey in 2010.

Otherness Being or feeling different in appearance or character from what is familiar, expected, or generally accepted.

Performative When a person or organisation participates in an activist movement not because they believe in the cause but they want the social capital that comes from doing it.

Prove it again bias When those from the global majority must work harder to establish competence.

Psychological safety The held belief that you will not suffer any negative consequences through taking interpersonal risks. Amy Edmondson coined the term "psychological safety" in 1999.

Race A social construct, a grouping system created by humans. Race was invented as a means of outlining physical differences between people, with one group classified as superior to another.

Racial fluency The fluency with which you can talk about race and ethnicity. The term was coined by Dr Doyin Atewologun in 2014.

Racial justice The systematic fair treatment of people of all races that results in equitable opportunities and outcomes for everyone.

Racial privilege The societal privilege that benefits white people over non-white people in some societies, particularly if they are otherwise under the same social, political, or economic circumstance.

Racial profiling The act of suspecting, targeting, or discriminating against a person on the basis of their ethnicity, religion, or nationality, rather than on individual suspicion or available evidence.

Racial prejudice An unjustified or incorrect attitude (usually negative) towards an individual based solely on the individual's membership of the global majority.

Racism Involves one group having the power to carry out systematic discrimination through the institutional policies and practices of the society and by shaping the cultural beliefs and values that support those racist policies and practices.

Stereotype   A racial stereotype is a depiction of an ethnicity or race, based on tropes and clichés. Stereotypes are harmful because they reduce the complexity of real people and erase individuality, agency, and power.

Sponsor   Someone who is an advocate for the global majority, provides stretch opportunities and shadowing, and talks about them positively in spaces they don't have access to.

Systemic/institutional racism   A form of racism that is embedded in the laws and regulations of a society or an organisation. It manifests as discrimination in areas such as criminal justice, employment, housing, health care, education, and political representation.

Tightrope bias   Pressure to behave in certain ways, if you go too far one way or the other there are penalties or a backlash, so you have a very narrow scope of acceptable behaviours.

Tokenism   The practice of making only minimal and symbolic gestures to be inclusive.

Unconscious bias   Social stereotyping about certain groups of people that individuals form outside of their own conscious awareness.

Whataboutery   When people protest about perceived inconsistency and refuse to act in one instance unless similar action is taken in other similar instances. For example, #BlackLivesMatter and #AllLivesMatter.

White passing   When someone perceives a person from the global majority as a white person. Some people from the global majority labelled white passing are viewed as having more privilege than other individuals in their community.

White supremacy   Refers to a social system in which white people enjoy structural advantages (privilege) over the global majority, on both a collective and individual level, despite even formal legal equality.

INDEX